Snapshots from the Journey

Recalling Moments of Relationship, Rescue, and Renewal

To Alicia and Donna Thank you for Celebrating the Journey of Jesus with me. In His Love, Becky Ps 37:4

BECKY CHENEY BURGUE

All Scripture quotations, unless otherwise indicated, are from the NEW INTERNATIONAL VERSION (NIV):Scripture taken from THE HOLY BIBLE, NEW INTERNATIONAL VERSION ®. Copyright©1973, 1978, 1984, 2011 by Biblica, Inc.™. Used by permission of Zondervan.

Scriptures marked NKJV are taken from the NEW KING JAMES VERSION (NKJV): Scripture taken from the NEW KING JAMES VERSION®. Copyright© 1982 by Thomas Nelson, Inc. Used by permission. All rights reserved.

Scriptures marked (NASB) are taken from the New American Standard Bible, © Copyright 1960, 1962, 1963, 1968, 1971, 1972, 1973, 1975, 1977, 1995 by the Lockman Foundation. Used by permission.

ISBN: 978-1-945975-56-1

Published by EA Books Publishing a division of Living Parables of Central Florida, Inc. a 501c3
EABooksPublishing.com

DEDICATION

This book is dedicated to my husband, Pete Burgue, who said anyone can write a book, so here's mine.

CONTENTS

ACKNOWLEDGMENTS

First and foremost I give glory to God, the Creator and Sustainer of my life and the Redeemer of my story.

I am thankful to my mom, who wrote her story.

I am thankful to my husband, Pete, for encouraging me to write mine.

I am thankful to my friends, who provided encouragement along the journey.

I am thankful to my children, who gave life to the stories.

And finally, I am thankful to everyone who ever asked me, "Do you have a book?"

Introduction

I come from . . .

- a Creator who cares and parents who were prepared;
- my dad's work ethic and my mom's service;
- well-worn pews and robed choirs;
- King James verses committed to memory and hidden in my heart;
- Sunday morning services and vacation Bible school summers;
- strong opinions and basic beliefs;
- patriotic pride, where home and family and love and legacy stand for something;
- Ohio cousin summers and lightening bug rings;
- the middle of sister-brother bookends;
- twin beds and shared bathrooms;
- root-beer-float circles and beef-and-noodle Sundays;
- fried mush and maple syrup to Cuban toast and café con leche;
- popcorn nights and bacon mornings;

- consistent classrooms, invested teachers, and inspiring colleagues;
- home economics and Future Homemakers of America;
- footprints in the sand and blunders turned to beauty;
- scrapbook pages and handwritten letters;
- journal pages and the fragrance of friendship; and
- pictures and possibilities.

These pages contain a collection of who I was, who I am, and who I am becoming. My guess is that we have some things in common. We are all much more alike than we are different. Our stories share common elements of relationship, rescue, and renewal.

The roles we play in relationship all create or contribute to a false sense of self. The child we used to be shaped the adult we continue to become. The expectations of family and friends formed our assumptions about ourselves. Because we saw that self-image as reality, we didn't realize we were living in a distorted understanding of self. Once the realization comes, it is difficult to change and allow our true self to emerge—because everyone expects us to act and react the way we always have. Change is hard, and that old familiar pattern has been our friend, as dysfunctional as it is. We have to let that friendship go.

We were designed for community. We all desire relationships, but sometimes satisfying that desire causes us to lose important pieces of ourselves. That's where the rescue comes in. I frequently need to be rescued from myself—my own destructive thoughts, my desire to please others at my own expense. I need to be rescued from repeating patterns that caused me pain in the past. Can you relate? The rescue takes us from the destructive path we were on to a brand-new view of ourselves. That view will only be clear when we are willing to be rescued, when we desire to reclaim our true self and move forward. Only then will we move toward the new possibilities available in renewal.

Have you experienced the need for renewal—the desire for a new start, a brand-new day, a blank journal page?

That renewal is not only necessary but also life-giving. Renewal provides us a chance to start over, to begin again with a clear vision of who we are and where we are headed. Renewal may come as a day-to-day process of slow but steady change, or it may come all at once as a radical breaking free from old habits and patterns and a completely new sense of who we are. Either way, being patient in the process and giving ourselves the permission to let go and begin again is revitalizing.

We all experience seasons that require recall and reflection. Many times we are simply too busy to appreciate the moments when they happen. My mantra has always been "Celebrate the journey; don't wait for the destination." Enjoy the "right now" and get all you can from it rather than waiting for something else to happen, or waiting to appreciate it later. I hope you will take the time to celebrate the journey with me through these stories, and then to reflect on your own journey and recognize your need for relationships, rescue, and renewal as a part of that process. Remember, it's never too late. Perhaps you will even be inspired to write your own stories.

My mom wrote her story and I'm glad she did. She wrote while she could still remember. She wrote before Alzheimer's stole her story. She inspired me to write mine. This collection of stories started out as a mere chronicling of life to be passed on to the family; I really didn't think anyone else would be interested. I began to realize, as I shared pieces of my story in talks and teachings, that others were listening and responding. There seemed to be a combination of unique and universal in each milestone moment I shared. Pieces of my stories resonated with others, who were inspired to look at snapshots from their own lives and enjoy the journey.

We each have a story that is both unique and universal. Our stories are a collection of snapshots from our lives. Pictures with all kinds of possibilities. I believe stories should be shared and savored. Each one has the potential to make a difference for the storyteller and the story receiver.

I write my stories with hope.

I hope you will find these snapshots of my life entertaining as well as thought provoking.

I hope you will find comfort and consolation as you read.

I hope you will find opportunities to reflect as you read.

I hope you will find joy as you celebrate the journey with me.

I hope you will find encouragement to see ordinary moments as extraordinary gifts.

Part 1
Relationship

noun: **relationship**; *plural noun*: **relationships**
re·la·tion·ship / rəˈlāsh(ə)nship

The way in which two or more concepts, objects, or people are connected, or the state of being connected.
　　synonyms: connection, relation, association, link, correlation, correspondence, parallel, alliance, bond, interrelation, interconnection

- The state of being connected by blood or marriage. *synonyms*: family ties, family connections, blood ties, blood relationship, kinship, affinity, consanguinity, common ancestry, common lineage

- The way in which two or more people or organizations regard and behave toward each other.

- an emotional and sexual association between two people. *synonyms:* romance, (love) affair, love, liaison, amour, partnership

We were created for community, connection, and alliance. We are designed to be in relationship with others. A baby is conceived because of the most intimate relationship of all and then born into a family where needs are met and love and trust are taught. So, literally, our lives are born of relationship and born for relationship. In that first relationship of family we learn how to relate to others and we learn about ourselves. Attachments, the formation of strong emotional ties, are created or perhaps denied in this initial family relationship, and this will affect the rest of our lives. That kinship can be applied or denied.

How about that synonym *consanguinity*? What a fun word to say, and it means having the same ancestry. Is that enough to constitute a relationship? So many people now have a greater desire to explore their genealogy. What are we looking for?

I love the portion of the above definition that talks about the way we regard and behave toward one another, indicating there is action to be observed, something tangible to receive from a relationship. We are all much more alike than we are different. We all want the same things. We all want to be heard and seen acknowledged and valued. We all want to know that we matter to someone. Those things would all be experienced in the context of a "real" relationship.

I hope as you read the stories of my relationships, you will reflect on your own. Relationships can be risky; hurt can be received and rendered. We must take responsibility for our role in the relationship. I hope you will take an honest inventory of the relationships in your life and what you have learned from them, identify any that need repair, and most importantly, look at any void that exists and how that void might be filled.

And let us consider how we may spur one another on toward love and good deeds, not giving up meeting together, as some are in the habit of doing, but encouraging one another—and all the more as you see the Day approaching.
Hebrews 10:24–25

Chapter 1
What I Know to Be True

My story began in Galion, Ohio, on November 11, 1952, at 9:58 a.m. in Galion City Hospital. I weighed 7 lbs, 11½ oz; was 20 inches long; and was born into a family including my proud parents, Mary L. Sherrard Cheney, thirty, and Richard Lee Cheney, thirty-one; one sister, Bonnie Lynn Cheney, seven; and a dog named Bootsie. I know this because others told me.

I was baptized on March 29, 1953, at First Presbyterian Church in Crestline, Ohio, by Reverend Gerald Palmer. I know this because I have a baptism certificate.

Before I was born, my father was in the army, stationed in Tampa, Florida, before being deployed to Germany. In April 1945 he lost his leg at the hand of a sniper and returned to the States, to his young bride and baby. They lived in Ohio until I was born in 1952, and on September 12, 1953, we left Ohio for Florida. I was ten months old. I know this because those same others told me.

My mother and father and sister made the trip with me, and when we arrived in Tampa, we stayed in a motel on Hillsborough Avenue. I know this because I have a picture.

Sept. 1953

I was an uncooperative traveler. In fact, I was labeled precocious and apparently have been living up to that label ever since. I know this because I heard the story over and over and over.

In October 1953, we bought a house at 522 E. Norfolk Street, where I lived until I went away to college in 1970. I know this because I have more pictures and lots of memories.

One of my earliest memories in this house was naptime in my parents' bedroom. I am not a napper now, nor have I ever been. I don't like to waste daylight. My mom would place me in the middle of the big double bed and shut the door. The bed seemed so high and the sheets always smelled like the outdoors. The wooden headboard had a pattern of carved bells that I traced over and over with my fingers, instead of sleeping. I now know it as the Liberty Bell pattern on the furniture my parents bought and paid for in installments, before they were married. I know this because I have their receipts.

When I sat in the middle of the bed I could see my reflection in the mirror of the dressing table. One day I saw my mother's purse on the stool of the dressing table. Leaning over the edge of the bed, I could just reach it, so I opened it and found her lipstick. I returned to the center of the big double bed and proceeded to use the lipstick to color my lips as I had seen my mother do many times. But I didn't stop with my lips—I covered my entire face with lipstick and admired myself in the mirror. My "naptime" was interrupted when Aunt Betty, my mother's younger sister visiting from Ohio, entered the room to find me covered with red lipstick, looking quite proud of myself. She called Uncle Howard to bring the camera to capture the moment. I remember my mother wasn't impressed, but she did save the picture! I know this because now I have that picture.

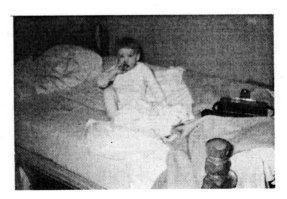

I knew how to whistle before I knew how to talk. I know this because everyone told me.

I went to preschool at Flora and Central Playground and my teacher was Mrs. Reba Haynes. I loved school and being with friends, but I was talkative and spent much of my time in the corner for talking or whistling in class. I know this because Mrs. Haynes told me.

My first day of first grade was traumatic. I know this because I actually remember.

It was September 1958 and I was six years old. My dress was ready, my shoes were ready, my black velvet purse with the little white poodle on the front was ready, and my father's cigar box with all my school supplies was ready, but I was not ready! We took a picture on the front porch and walked to Cleveland Elementary to meet Mrs. Charlotte Eden. When I say "we," I mean my father and me. My mom wasn't home because she was in the hospital with my new baby brother. I hadn't even met him yet and already didn't like him. I know this because I have the hospital menus with my mother's notes written on the back, notes that said she missed me and knew I would be a great big sister.

When my mother and new baby brother came home, Benjamin Lyle Cheney, the brother I heard so much about, was finally real. He was tiny and yellow from jaundice, and I was afraid to touch him, but my mom encouraged me to sit in a chair and hold him in my lap. I know this because I remember, and I have a picture too.

 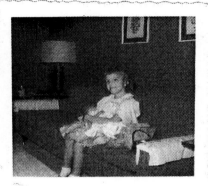

Our memories are filled with a combination of what we actually remember and what we've heard and seen in photo albums. Have you ever noticed how several people can live in the same house for a lot of years and have completely different views of what happened there? Family gatherings, where memories are shared, can become fertile ground for intense arguments about what happened and how we remember it. We can learn to accept and appreciate the differences in age, stage, and perception that explain why we don't recall things the same. We can treasure life as we remember it.

Do you have vivid memories of moments from the past? Do you have siblings whose memories are completely different of the same events? Do you have photo albums filled with memorable moments, or perhaps more realistically, boxes of photos with no names or dates that challenge your memory? Take the time to reflect on what you know to be true and why you know it, and stash those memories away where you know they'll be safe. These reflections can lead to a much greater truth and a truly safe place to put your trust and confidence. All our discoveries lead to the greatest discovery—that our only real confidence is in a God who never changes and will always lead us to the truth. Have you discovered He has a plan for your life?

Father, You are the creator and sustainer of our lives and of our amazing brains that have the capacity to store and organize memories. Give us the ability to remember and treasure the times we have enjoyed and even those times that were tough, knowing You have a perfect plan and purpose for all that we have experienced. Thank you most of all for Jesus. Amen.

Chapter 2
Parents Are People Too

Richard Lee Cheney and Mary Louise Sherrard were people before they became my parents.

My parents were people who lived in Columbus, Ohio, and attended school and church together. The schools were McKinley Junior High and North High. The church was Hansburger Memorial Methodist Church.

My parents were people with a strong work ethic evident in every season of their lives. They worked as teens—Mary was a server at the Vernors ginger ale stand at Ohio State University stadium and Richard worked for his father, Wendell, at George Byers New and Used Cars. They both continued to work as adults—Mary as a homemaker first and then a school food service worker and school cafeteria manager, and Richard in real estate, insurance, and local politics.

My parents were people with a lot in common. Their parents were divorced. They both lived with their moms, Lydia Cheney and Mildred Sherrard, who loved them and sacrificed in order to provide for them.

My parents were both quite shy and enjoyed school and church. They wrote letters—lots of letters to each other—and I still treasure every one. My mother had them all stored in a large manila envelope, which I now have. Included are notes from junior high and high school from Richard to Mary, questioning her about love and loyalty—he needed to know he was her one and only.

My parents were people who fell in love and got engaged on August 31, 1940, Mary's eighteenth birthday.

My parents were people who planned. In March of 1941 they purchased a new home on a land contract, a form of seller financing where the payments are made to the seller instead of to a bank or mortgage company, since they weren't old enough to finance it in their own names. The address was 1746 East Kenworth Road, Columbus, Ohio, and the house looks much the same today as it did in 1941. It cost $4,150 and they paid $350 down and $41.50 monthly. They also bought their furniture and had it all paid off by their wedding day.

Then   Now

My parents were people who believed in commitment. On June 28, 1941, she wore a beautiful wedding dress she made herself. The wedding party consisted of my aunts and their husbands. Family and friends witnessed their vows, with Reverend E. S. Matheny of the Community Church in Columbus presiding. My parents made a promise to be partners through it all—in sickness and in health, til death—and they made good on that promise.

My parents were people who sacrificed. Their wedding reception was at the home of Mary's mother, Mildred, who made all the food herself. There was no honeymoon since they had spent all of their money on their home and furniture. They lived in that home when Richard went into the army in 1943 and when my sister, Bonnie, was born on November 21, 1945. My father returned home as an amputee on November 23, 1945. His letters from war were precious and always positive, each of them signed, "All my Love, all my life."

Richard spent some time at Walter Reed Hospital learning to adjust with the other amputees, and his contagious smile and love for life was an inspiration to the other young men who had also sacrificed limbs.

In 1950 my parents moved to Galion, Ohio, where I was born in 1952, and the next year we all moved to Tampa,

Florida. My brother was born six years later and our family was complete.

My parents were people who understood family and community commitment. They chaperoned school functions, served on the PTA, and never missed one of our important events. They taught Sunday school and served in the church. They were tithers and taught us to be the same. My father was the superintendent of Sunday school and the church treasurer, and my mother was the nursery worker and president of the Presbyterian Women; we could all be found at North Tampa Presbyterian Church every time the doors were open.

My parents were patriotic people who loved this country and never missed an election and the opportunity to make their voice known with a vote. My father was a politician in the best sense of the word, and I love politics because of him. He served on the Tampa City Council and was acting mayor of Tampa when he died of a massive heart attack at the age of fifty-two. My mother lived another thirty-six years without him, dying at age eighty-eight with Alzheimer's. He was the one and only love of her life as she was his, and there was never a question of the love and loyalty they shared.

As a result of the promise they made to be partners for a lifetime, they became parents. I never want to forget that they were people first, and the people they were before made them the parents they became. They were parents who taught by example and who loved each other and their children well. They were parents who provided a stable, consistent, loving home. They were parents with a strong sense of community and a devoted love for the Lord. They were parents who left a rich and lasting legacy, and for that I am forever grateful.

Treasure hunt the experiences of your childhood and take the time to see your parents or guardians as people—people who weren't perfect but who contributed to the person you are today. We may strive to be exactly like them or completely different, but the reality is usually somewhere in between.

Do you have a heritage you are proud of? If so, treasure the legacy and commit to passing it on those you love. Perhaps you don't have such a heritage. If that's the case, how will you change that cycle and be sure you leave a legacy of love? Parents do the best they can with what they know and have. There are no perfect parents and no perfect children, so in accepting that truth and moving on from there, we must be kind and forgiving to ourselves and to our parents.

Father, You are the Father who will never leave or forsake us. You are the only perfect one. You are the giver of grace, mercy, and forgiveness. Teach us to do that for others in our lives. Show us where we need to forgive and where we need to be forgiven. We are grateful for the legacy we each have been given. Guide us as we leave a positive, godly legacy for those who come after us. Thank you most of all for Jesus. Amen.

Chapter 3
A Legacy of Faith

*Therefore **we** also, since **we** are surrounded by so great a cloud of witnesses, let **us** lay aside every weight, and the sin which so easily ensnares **us**, and let **us** run with endurance the race that is set before **us**, looking unto Jesus, the author and finisher of **our** faith.*

Hebrews 12:1–2, NKJV (emphasis mine)

I have had the occasion recently to reflect on the meaning of this verse and implication of just who **we**, **us**, and **our** might represent.

I have always been well aware of the faith legacy my parents left me, but I had the desire to dig a little deeper and see who else had a part in my foundation of faith.

My father, Richard Lee Cheney, born December 21, 1921, was a man of great character and strength and unshakable faith. He died on June 20, 1974, at the early age of fifty-two. The life and legacy lesson from him: we can't wait to sow the seeds of faith; we don't know how much time we have.

His parents, Wendell M. Cheney and Lydia Stotler Cheney, were part of my life—Wendell for a brief eight years and Lydia for twenty-eight years. They were divorced long before I was born, and that was a strange concept for me to grasp as a child. Wendell died early also, of heart disease, at the age of fifty-eight. My father's grandparents were Ralph L. Cheney and Maude Mae Shadwick.

Seated on the Liberty Bell bed my parents bought before they were married, looking through an old scrapbook my mother put together, I found an article about my great-grandfather, Ralph L. Cheney. The article was a *Who's Who in Linden* and spoke of his contribution to the small Ohio community. I read with interest and learned he had been a teacher for nine years and then a lawyer and then acting police justice. Another legacy lesson came as I read about his teaching tenure and his service to the community: the heart for service I had seen in my father and now possess myself was a gift passed down through the generations.

An obituary I found revealed that Ralph died at the age of fifty-seven from heart disease, much the same as his son, Wendell, and grandson, Richard. He was a lawyer and a Republican and loved the outdoors. There was no mention of his teaching or his faith in his obituary. His wife, Maude Mae Shadwick, lived to be seventy-six. She was a housewife and a midwife. I learned she gave birth to six children, including two who died at birth, one of whom was a twin. Perhaps her birth experiences caused her to become a midwife and help others in the birthing process. Another legacy lesson: circumstances of life may happen so we recognize trials in our lives and can then help others with the same or similar struggles.

Maude's parents were Lafayette Shadwick and Sarah Bell Hunter. Lafayette died in 1899, which is all I could discover about him. Sarah Bell Hunter, however, is a different story. She is, I am certain, among that *"great cloud of witnesses."*

Sarah Bell Hunter Shadwick, seated; (l-r) Mary Belle Cheney
Helser, granddaughter; Maude Mae Shadwick Cheney, daughter;
and Mary Kathryn Helser Bohyer (family friend)

Ralph Lee Cheney and Maude Mae Shadwick on their wedding
day, April 2, 1896

According to Sara Bell's obituary:

Sarah Bell Hunter was the daughter of Martha and Samuel
Hunter. She was born January 26, 1853, and departed this
life March 22, 1942, at the age of 89 years, one month, and
24 days. She was united in marriage to Lafeyette Shadwick
in Jefferson, Iowa, on November 25, 1874. To this union
were born nine children, five having preceded her in the

23

slumber of death. She is survived by two daughters, Mrs. Maude Cheney; Mrs. Mattie Banner, both of Columbus, Ohio; two sons, Orin of Blacklick, and Harry of the home; two sisters, Mrs. Ida Elliott, Vancouver, BC, and Anna Coleman, Kansas; 19 grandchildren and 20 great grandchildren.

She yielded her life to the Lord and affiliated with Christian Union at Havens Corners.

She came to Ohio and spent the remaining days of her life in and around Columbus, Ohio.

To her family and children she was a devoted mother. The light of Mother has gone out of this life, but the light she has left burning in each loved one's heart will be a beacon light guiding their footsteps until that grand homecoming. They will meet her and her smile of welcome waiting, where there is no night, and will meet you with a glad good morning.

I like that, especially those terms *yielded, affiliated, devoted,* and *beacon.* We don't write like that or talk like that anymore, which I find to be a shame.

I will continue this journey of discovery, examining and recording my life, because, as Emerson observed, "The unrecorded life is not worth examining."

Each of us will leave a legacy and each of us carries a part of the legacy left for us. Many of us will realize and cherish that legacy while others may not even be aware they are part of a much bigger story. We may never know some of the ancestral connections that contributed to who we are today, but that doesn't make them any less important. When we do get a glimpse of the past and its bearing on the present, we can be thankful and make an intentional choice to continue to learn and then teach these legacy lessons.

Thank you, great-great grandmother, Sarah Bell Hunter, for the faith foundation you began over one hundred years ago. Your light still shines, and some glad morning I will meet you on that celestial shore.

Do you know much about your family history? I don't want to be obsessed with digging into genealogy but I do appreciate the stories that have been shared and the interesting facts I've found. Are you aware of the legacy you are leaving? We all influence others whether we are aware of it or not. Someone is always watching. What do you want them to see? What do you hope they will remember? Are you leaving a legacy of faith or fear?

Father, You are the redeemer and the One who restores our story. Give us a desire to live our lives in light of what You have done for us. Cause us to live like we have been redeemed and restored. Give us opportunities to share that story with others. Help us to be a positive influence on others and to leave marks of Your love on their lives. We are able to love because You loved us first. Thank you most of all for Jesus. Amen.

Chapter 4
Childhood Chores

Childhood chores have a way of providing structure and security to a young life. When I was young, chores were expected of each family member and certainly weren't tied to allowance. There was no payment for chores; they were the responsibility of all in the house who benefitted from being part of the family. Those benefits included a roof over my head, a bed to sleep in, and three, as my mother called them, square meals a day.

My favorite childhood chore was ironing, and to this day I love to iron. (I know, some people think I'm crazy.) There was a special space in our house dedicated to this chore and a window to look out on the world as I ironed. It was quite a ritual to prepare items for ironing. My mom had a glass Coca-Cola bottle with a cap with holes in it. I filled the bottle with water and sprinkled the items to be ironed—pillowcases, napkins, tablecloths, handkerchiefs, and of course, items of clothing. After sprinkling them with water, I rolled them and placed them in the refrigerator for a time. Later, I took them out one at a time and ironed them, being careful to remove every wrinkle. The moisture from the sprinkling provided a steam action, since there were no steam irons back then. The completed item was then carefully folded and placed in the drawer or on the shelf in the linen closet, or hung on a hanger on the handle of the cabinet door until it was placed in the appropriate closet.

Ironing followed a predictable pattern, with steps to follow. This chore gave me a feeling of safety and security. I even ironed on vacation. (While other kids were looking for the pool, one of the first things I checked in a hotel room was the closet, looking for the iron and ironing board.) In ironing, I found satisfaction in a job well done, a chore successfully completed.

When I learned to sew, carefully pressing the seams at each stage of the garment construction was the key to a finished, professional look. Wow, I would love for my mom to hear me make that statement now. She drilled it into my head during our sewing sessions, and she always knew when I tried to skip the pressing step.

As a teen and college student I made most of my own clothes. As a young mom I made outfits for my children, who always had the best homemade Halloween costumes. I felt a great deal of pride in a job well done, and skipping steps or trying to save time by cutting out the pressing of seams would be evident in the finished product.

A childhood chore is a picture of the bigger things in life. The Bible says he who is faithful in a little will be faithful in much (Luke 16:10). If you can be trusted to do the chore well without skipping steps, then maybe you can be trusted with more responsibility. The way you approach the tedious and often mundane details of a task will show in the final outcome. My time spent in those methodical steps of ironing taught me to appreciate those details. It also gave me time to contemplate the bigger things in life. Remember, I had my window to the world right in front of me to make the most of every minute. A sloppy job or an attitude of "This can't possibly be important, so I'll skip it" would show up in the end.

The same is true of the way I approach life and all its tedious and often mundane details. I love the safety and security of a step-by-step process, knowing that each step is critical to the success of the final product. I learned that love is in the details, and every phase of the task at hand has a purpose. I live my life in the comfort of routine, and if one hasn't been previously established, I will create one. However, I am not so routine-oriented that I can't find time to explore new opportunities and celebrate the journey.

What makes you feel safe and secure? Even those who are less comfortable with schedules and more spontaneous in nature need a sense of order in life to feel secure. In what ways have you learned the importance of carefully completing each step and not compromising or cutting corners to save time or other resources? What lessons did you learn from childhood chores? Do you feel that sense of safety and security still today as you complete that childhood chore?

Father, You are the creator of order and safety and security in our lives. You give patience and perseverance for the tedious parts of our lives and the details of our days that can be exasperating and may tempt us to cut corners or skip steps. Teach us that the process is important. Teach us to be faithful in the little things and help us model that faithfulness for those who are watching us. Thank you most of all for Jesus. Amen.

Chapter 5
The Family Table

I lived in the same house all my growing up years—the house I called home. While the house number changed when "the highway" came through and took all the houses on the street except three, not much else changed over the years. Our family of five—Mom, Dad, older sister, younger brother, and I—lived a consistent, controlled life. My mom believed in routine and ritual, which while comforting at times bordered on boring. Our most exciting days were holidays when family and friends joined us at the family table for a meal that wasn't on the weekly dinner schedule.

When you opened our front door you could see all the way through to the back door, and children immediately saw this layout as a racetrack that passed through the living room, the dining room, and the kitchen, and then curved through the utility room, my bedroom, the hall, and back into the living room. This pattern provided hours of fun for visiting cousins and neighbor children. However, on holidays that predictable pathway was interrupted by the presence of our grand family table, which was usually up against the dining room window with the sides down, taking up as little space as possible. On these special occasions, the beautiful, cherry gate-leg table was opened to full capacity with both leaves added.

That table has always intrigued me. It was one of the pieces of furniture my parents purchased on layaway the year before they were married. Though only teenagers, they were planners who knew what they wanted. I loved to listen to my mom tell the stories of the furniture. She would get that faraway look in her eye and her smile seemed brighter.

When that special table was opened for holiday meals, it took up the entire dining room. The upholstered chairs with no arms were positioned at opposite ends, and every other chair in the house was brought to the dining room for family and friends—the maple chairs from the breakfast room, the folding chairs from the back closet, and even the sewing machine chair. If there was a small child that particular year, then the kitchen stool doubled as a high chair at the table. These chairs were as unique as the people who sat in them. In preparation for a holiday meal, the cherry table, in all its grandeur, was covered with a protective table pad and two cloth tablecloths. Most guests never knew that beautiful table was under there.

Out came the silver and the china and the beautiful silver leaf glasses, which were used only on these special occasions. We did eat on dishes every night—no paper plates in this house—but they were known as everyday dishes and were stored in the breakfast room corner cabinet. The dishes used to set the holiday table came from the dining room china cabinet.

Preparations often started early the day before, and tantalizing smells wafted through the house from the kitchen, where my mother stood for hours. Our kitchen was nothing fancy like you see today—just two walls with a sink centered on one wall and the stove, counter, and refrigerator on the other—but that didn't stop my mom from working her magic there every day. In that simple kitchen she prepared meals that were consistently, routinely seasoned with love. Remembering it now makes me long for the comfort of knowing what to expect.

As time for the holiday meal drew near, the family table was filled with special dishes and serving pieces, large platters of food, depending on the holiday, but always traditional fare. With the family table set and laden with food, and the guests gathered, my father always delivered the blessing, thanking God for His abundant gifts of family, food, and fellowship. I always sat on the backside of the table in the middle seat, looking at the big mirror that hung above the cherry sideboard. I could see myself and the whole scene from there.

The house I called home has been sold, and mom gone on to her heavenly home. Most of those relatives who gathered around that table have also passed on as well, but they each left a legacy of love and faith for me. That cherry gate-leg table now occupies a spot in my house, and I never cover it with a protective pad. The matching cherry mirror hangs on the wall in the loft in my home now, and when I walk by it I sometimes catch a glimpse of that holiday gathering in the first house I called a home. What I wouldn't give to walk back through that front door and see those familiar faces welcoming me to the family table once again.

You may have your own family memories of holiday dinners or special times that made the usual feel exceptional. Perhaps you don't have memories because these times didn't exist in your life. You may have longed for these times around a family table and you may still long for them. It's not too late. What traditions around the table will you continue to observe? What traditions do you long for that you will begin to observe? What is that longing really about? It probably isn't the food or the table decorations. It's more about the people that gather and linger as if they don't want to leave. It's more about knowing that when they do leave they take something with them and also leave something behind. I hope you know and have experienced that feeling and that you allow yourself some time to reflect on what it all really means.

Father, You are the provider of every good and perfect gift. Thank you for times of celebration that cause us to want to linger longer and for that longing You put in our hearts for connection and community. Cause us to recall the memories of the past and to eagerly anticipate memories still to be made. Open our eyes to see the opportunities You give us each day. Thank you most of all for Jesus. Amen.

Chapter 6
Friendship Frames Life's Best Pictures

A friend loves at all times.
Proverbs 17:17

I have been blessed by the gift of friendship throughout my life. I am grateful for that gift and the comfort and security it continues to provide, as well as the precious memories it has left.

My parents set the example for me when it came to forming and preserving friendships. My mother and father were both friendly, social people and I watched them with their friends throughout the years. They had many couple friends as well as individual friendships they spent intentional time nurturing. I can remember vividly them going to church socials with other couples. Many of those occasions required theme dressing and supporting the ideas and causes of their friends. No wonder I love a theme party and will quickly jump on the bandwagon for a worthy cause today.

My mother especially taught me the value of maintaining and nurturing lifelong and often long-distance friendships. Moving from Ohio, my parents left many of their close friends and neighbors, which meant making an intentional effort to maintain those long-distance relationships. Therefore, my mother wrote letters often to her friends and taught me to do the same. Some of my most treasured times together with her were the times we spent sitting at the dining room table writing letters, and of course sending the annual Christmas cards, each containing a handwritten letter—no mass-produced Christmas letter ever went out from the Cheney family!

I watched my mother celebrate life's occasions with all her friends, even from a distance. Birthdays, anniversaries, Christmas, the births of new babies, and graduations were always acknowledged. Whether long distance or local, her longtime friends in Ohio and her newer friends in Tampa were a priority for my mother, and she constantly and lovingly nurtured those friendships for decades.

In her later years, only a few of her longtime friends were still living, but the devotion between them remained. They made nightly phone calls. Visiting on the porch switched to visiting at the hospital, rehab centers, or nursing homes. Handwritten cards and notes still kept them close, whether mailed or hand delivered.

One of the saddest things I had to face during my mom's Alzheimer's was when she could no longer write those notes or sign her name. I would still get out the notepaper and write the notes and sign her name for her, even though the notes were tear stained. Two of her lifelong friends continued to visit, and we would frequently talk on the way out of the facility about how hard it was that she didn't know them. Even so, they continued to visit, because they still knew her and loved her.

I love my friends and attempt to nurture friendships the way I was taught through my mother's lifelong example. I have several friends I meet with weekly and others I talk to on the phone weekly. My college roommate and fellow home economics major is my longest-lasting friendship. I met Christy at FSU in 1971 and we lived together with several other girls and a house manager in the Home Management House—a course requirement for all home economics majors.

Dorothy Sidwell, smoking
at the table

Pam, me, Christy, Nell

Pam, Mary, Linda, me, Christy

Christy and I were in each other's first weddings—though both ended in divorce. We were a solace for one another when our fathers died. We continued to maintain a long-distance friendship, despite the forty years she was in Los Angeles and my return to Tampa after college graduation.

I have every letter and card Christy has sent for the past four decades, and that was the primary way we communicated all those years. If I received a phone call from her, it meant she was in town or something bad happened, and a phone call from me to her was for the same reasons. We love writing letters and sending cards. We don't email, Facebook, or tweet—it just wouldn't be the same. We have seen each other thorough divorce, death, birth, adoption, surgery, disease, the growing pains of our children, career changes, and downsizing.

Once we both retired, I prayed Christy would move back to Florida so we could have frequent face-to-face time doing what we love. That prayer has been answered, and now she is just thirty minutes away and we are intentional about spending a day together every week. We both love thrifting and antiquing, so a weekly treasure hunt with my lifelong friend is a picture I love taking. I have the frames ready—probably bought at a thrift shop.

We were designed for community, and those precious friendships serve a greater purpose in our lives. Friends love us enough to tell us the truth and keep us accountable. A friendship that stands the test of time is truly a treasure. When we have been through the good, the bad, and the ugly together, we can pick up right where we left off, and that is an advantage of intentional, sometimes hard-fought, friendships.

Friendship looks different to different people—to some it is a constant companion and to others it is just knowing someone is there when you need them. The adage "In order to have a friend, you must be a friend" is truth. I would like to believe I am the kind of friend I long to have. What kind of friend are you? Do you have precious and lifelong friends? What has been your main method of communication through the years? Have you let them know how important they are? Are you intentional about taking the time to nurture those friendships? Take the time now to write a note or make a call and arrange to spend some treasured time together.

Father, You have designed us for community and blessed us with friends to share our joys and sorrows. You have provided friends to get us through the tough times. Friends who are faithful to point us to You and to pray with us. Friends who hold our arms up when we don't have the strength, and in turn we do the same for them. I am so thankful for those relationships you have placed in my life. Help me to be sensitive to the needs of others and in turn to trust them with my needs. Thank you most of all for Jesus. Amen.

Chapter 7
A 1 Corinthians 13 Love

I have been blessed with a I Corinthians kind of love.

Love is patient.
1 Corinthians 13:4

My husband, Peter Burgue Jr., is the kindest, most generous, most patient man I know. He is the only child of parents, Zenaida and Pedro Burgue Sr., and he was born September 15, 1951, and raised in Tampa, Florida. I watched him patiently care for his aging mom, and I have experienced his patience firsthand as he deals with my daily "Let's do it now" mentality.

Love is kind.
1 Corinthians 13:4

We met in 1974 while working for the City of Tampa Recreation Department, at Oak Park Playground. I noticed his kindness in the way he worked with the children on the playground and senior adults in the center. He truly cared about others and he demonstrated that care with acts of service. His love language is acts of service, and he does them with a kindness clearly felt by each recipient. In addition to the fact that he was tall, dark, and handsome, I was attracted to his heart, the twinkle in his eyes, and a smile that could melt my heart.

After asking my mother for my hand in marriage, we became engaged on February 14, 1976, at CK's revolving restaurant at the Tampa International Airport, and we celebrated many anniversaries there. Our wedding invitation stated:

"As the sun starts a new day, so our love begins a new life!"

Love does not envy, it does not boast, it is not proud.
1 Corinthians 13:4

We were married on July 10, 1976, in the backyard, on the lake of the home we would later buy and live in to this day. It was a humble ceremony in a beautiful unpretentious setting. We stood side by side, attended by my sister and Pete's cousin, surrounded by a small, intimate group of family and friends. I wore a yellow dress my mother made, and Pete wore a powder-blue Johnny Carson suit.

Love does not delight in evil but rejoices with the truth.
1 Corinthians 13:6

David R. Holt performed the ceremony, and Joe Dill sang *I Believe* and *The Hawaiian Wedding Song* while we stood side by side and made a promise first to God and then to each other. The truth of God's Word was clearly proclaimed in the ceremony and has always been the foundation of our marriage. To rejoice means to be full of joy, to feel gladness. This is not referring to the fleeting happiness people often say they want; it is a deep abiding joy that cannot by diminished by any circumstances. Our marriage has proven that love truly does rejoice in and because of the truth.

Love does not dishonor others, it is not self-seeking, it is not easily angered, it keeps no record of wrongs.
1 Corinthians 13:5

We went to Hawaii on our honeymoon, but we weren't alone. My mother, brother, sister, and the entire Tampa delegation to the 1976 National School Food Service Association were with us. Believe me, there were plenty of opportunities to be rude or to demand to have it your way. This was truly a test of patience and endurance. It was also Pete's first plane flight. Now, that's love!

We moved into our home at 5624 Half Moon Lake Road, Tampa, Florida, in time for our first Christmas together, December 1976. I believe love is in the dailies not just the milestone moments. Our dailies were and continue to be consistent and comfortable, safe and secure in the knowledge of an enduring love.

Struggles lay ahead of us but:

Love always protects, always trusts, always hopes, and always perseveres.
1 Corinthians 13:7

The seasons of life have brought change and circumstances that required persistence, patience, and plenty of prayer. We have faced infertility and my hysterectomy at age twenty-seven, with Pete praying in the waiting room and writing a love letter I will always treasure. We ventured into the uncharted territory of adoption together and were blessed with a daughter first, and a son two years later.

March 7, 1983

We weathered the storms of heart problems with our son and a life-threatening eating disorder with our daughter, when she was a teen. We experienced being caregivers for our mothers, who were both widowed before we married. We have celebrated milestone moments, and I remember our twenty-fifth anniversary and feeling blessed beyond what I could have imagined.

July 10, 2001

We grieved the deaths of our mothers and taught our children how to grieve not "as others who have no hope" (1 Thessalonians 4:13). We celebrated our daughter's marriage and then grieved her divorce. We encouraged our son through two deployments in the navy and experienced the pride of the Tiger Cruise on his return home. We celebrated our son's marriage to the girl of his dreams and gained a daughter-in-law we adore. We transitioned into retirement after long and satisfying careers: thirty-eight years with the City of Tampa Recreation Department for Pete, and thirty-six years with the Hillsborough County School system for me.

We do not know what the future holds, and the past certainly didn't turn out the way we would have written it, but we will "press on toward the goal to win the prize for which God has called [us] heavenward in Christ Jesus" (Philippians 3:14).

Now these three remain: faith, hope, and love. But the greatest of these is love.
1 Corinthians 13:13

Scriptures like 1 Corinthians 13 speak into our lives in ways we can't imagine, and they speak to us differently in different seasons of our lives. Think of all the times in your life when you've had opportunities to give and receive love. Love is not limited to marital or romantic love—it is much bigger than that. This may be a good exercise for you, to take this scripture apart phrase by phrase and see how it has and continues to apply to all your relationships.

The model of all relationships is the one we have with God our Father. He loves us more than we can fathom and teaches us how to fully love one another. How do you give and receive love? Do you find yourself comparing your life to others and wishing you had the kind of love they have? Pray that you will be a pure vessel for God's love to flow through to others He has placed in your life, and pray prayers of thanksgiving for those who have demonstrated His love to you.

Father, You are the One who loves us completely and unconditionally. You are the example of truth and love. Help us to love one another as You love us. Empty us of ourselves and fill us with Your love and compassion. Thank you for those who have faithfully shared Your love with us. Thank you for those You have placed in our lives that we might love them the way You love us. Thank you most of all for Jesus. Amen.

Chapter 8
A Pet Story

As a child I didn't have pets. I vaguely remember hearing of a family dog that died before I was born, so maybe that was the reason. I do recall a pet rabbit as a teenager but that didn't last long.

Pete had a dog as a young boy so he wanted us to have one. Our first dog as a married couple was a Chihuahua named Holly. Pete gave her to me in a Christmas stocking and I was surprised and delighted.

Holly was not the temperament of a "typical" Chihuahua, hyper and yappy; she was calm and quiet—it seemed she had taken on the temperament of our home at the time. My mother-in-law, Zenaida, had Holly's sister, Tiny, who was a typical Chihuahua.

Holly was a delight and a joy and brought me hours of pleasure and comfort. I could tell her anything and everything and my secrets were safe with her. She knew when I was sick or sad and sensed the need for soothing and solace. She endured being dressed in fuzzy footies that I had altered to become dog sweaters, since she was too small for any available in the pet stores. She even learned to share our love and affection when the children came along. I remember vividly a conversation I had with her before we adopted Christina. It went something like this:

> *Holly, things are getting ready to change drastically around here. A baby is coming to live with us, and she will need lots of love and attention. You were here first and we love you very much and we know you are going to love her very much too.*

The day we brought Christina home, Holly reacted as if she knew this was the "baby" I had been preparing her for. She approached her carefully and sniffed her curiously and then curled up beside me with her new sister. When Peter came along two years later, she was ready and he was her boy. My favorite picture of them together is one where she is as close as she can get to his back as he is sitting on the floor watching TV. She lived much longer than the typical Chihuahua, sixteen years, and I am convinced it was because of all the love.

Sadly, Christina came home from middle school one day to find Holly on the dining room floor with a broken neck—she had fallen from the second-story loft. Holly's fall had been due to aging, failing eyesight, and arthritis in her hind legs. We took her to the vet and she had to be "put to sleep." That was one of our most difficult days as a family. The ride home was spent in total silence except for the separate sobs of each of the four of us. I remember no one wanted to go back into the house, which seemed at the time like it could never be home again without Holly. I knew I never wanted to feel that way again, so that meant never having another dog.

A few years later Christina was struggling with anorexia, and weekly counseling sessions were part of our routine. Returning home from one of those sessions, we saw a sign on the side of Lakeshore Drive that read "Free puppies." We pulled over and a puppy picked us! We came home with a little black Doberman-Rottweiler mix that we named Lady. She quickly became the new light of our home, and everyone immediately fell in love with her—even Pete, who said he didn't want another dog and we should take her back. By that night he was her daddy, the official dog walker and primary caregiver.

He still was to the day, sixteen years later, as she struggled with cancer and renal failure. We faced the same feelings we had before of how to let go. The big difference this time was that we already had another dog, a four-year-old Bichon Frise, Annie. She was a joy and delight and she loved Lady. It was hard to imagine one without the other. I had to have those talks with Annie attempting to prepare her—and me—for what seemed inevitable. Lady died a natural death at home, and we were thankful we didn't have to make the decision to have her put down. Annie still sniffed her bed and came to me for comfort while at the same time giving comfort.

We now have a second dog, Gidget, a Yorkie-poo who provides both pleasure and irritation to Annie, and our holidays are now graced with our grand-dogs, Kal and Snoopy. They give a love that can't be described, and these two are truly a case of who rescued who when you see the way our son and daughter-in-love relate to them.

Each dog has had a special place in the family and a unique relationship with each of the humans in the house. They were always waiting at the door and gave an exuberant greeting when we came home. During family evenings they seemed to rotate laps, knowing they needed to give love equally, or it could have just been according to who still had popcorn in their bowl. Peter had his dog that needed a boy, and Christina had her dog that liked to be dressed. I had cuddle time with all of them when everyone else was gone. And Pete, well, he's always been the official walker and keeper of the treats, so it goes without saying that he was and still is every dog's favorite. Our pets and grand-pets are the best givers of unconditional love—no back talk, no arguing, just sloppy kisses, pulling your hand back with their paw for more petting, and begging for belly rubs.

Pets bring pleasure and awaken passion that we cannot imagine, and losing one brings pain that can't be predicted or prevented.

What childhood pet memories have influenced your pet ownership decisions as an adult? Can you recall a time when a pet brought you comfort like no human could? How do you remember the unconditional love you received from that canine or feline member of the family? Have you given yourself permission to grieve the loss of a pet that you loved?

Father, You are the creative designer of all that we enjoy. You have blessed us with pets that enrich our lives and give us the opportunity to extend and receive love. We are grateful for the love they bring and even for the sorrow we feel when they are no longer with us. That sorrow serves to remind us how deep our affection was for them. Keep us ever mindful that all we have is from You. Thank you most of all for Jesus. Amen.

Chapter 9
Focus on the Family

Family photos through the years can tell quite a story of together times for celebrations and milestone moments, but while a picture may be worth a thousand words, there is always a story behind the picture.

The first family photo I have is of Mom and Dad; my sister, Bonnie; my baby brother, Ben; and me on the couch in our home. This was the home we would live in all of my life, the home my mother continued to live in until 1999. My mother and father both had difficult and inconsistent lives as children, and I believe that's why they were so determined to provide us with a consistent, safe, and secure life in one place. I also believe that might have something to do with why they wanted to move from Ohio to Florida—to be physically and emotionally removed from their painful pasts.

The distance was a breaking free of sorts, though it was obvious my parents both loved their families and wanted to stay connected. Aunts, uncles, cousins, and grandparents came to Florida for visits, and every summer we would drive "straight through" to Ohio to visit the relatives. I loved those visits—houses with basements were so much fun, and being with cousins at the county fair was always a highlight. We stayed at Grandma Burns's house, my mother's mother, and I spent almost all of my time there in the basement ironing anything I could find on the mangle ironing machine—it was my favorite thing to do.

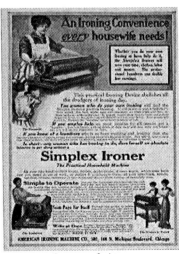

(mangle)

While in Columbus we always visited my aunts and uncles. My mother's two older sisters, Betty and Dorothy, were very different and I found those differences intriguing. Aunt Dorothy was the secretary to the mayor of Columbus and she always took me to city hall and then shopping downtown. My Aunt Betty was feisty and fabulous, in my book. I liked her and she liked me, but my mom wasn't happy about that. I think Aunt Betty represented her alter ego, the things my mom may have wanted to do or say but would have never dared. I always knew when my mom said, "You're just like your Aunt Betty" that it wasn't a compliment!

My mom ended up having three children, and though it wasn't planned that way, there were seven years between each of us, and my brother was definitely a surprise. Mom's sisters both only had one child—Dorothy had one son, Doug; Betty had one daughter, Patty. Divorce was not something my mom or her sisters experienced, and I'm sure that's what they hoped for their children. However, family pictures tell a story of five children and seven divorces, not exactly the example that had been set for us.

My father's sister, Doris, and her husband, Dave, were special to me- I loved visiting their house and staying in the loft room. Aunt Doris made the best key lime pie and Uncle Dave had installed a beer tap that came right out of the kitchen sink. They had two sons, Mike and Chuck.

Our annual summer visits to Columbus were split between my relatives' houses, spending time together, eating, and playing games. There were no expensive theme parks or restaurant meals, just simple country summer fun. When the time came for me to have my own family, I was determined we would take great family vacations doing something each of us wanted to do rather than visiting relatives, but remembering those summers now, those vacations weren't so bad after all.

My dad's father, Wendell, lived in Crestline and ran the family business, Cheney Motors. I remember the drive from Columbus to Crestline (over sixty miles) and the anticipation of seeing their beautiful house. Wendell had been married several times but the only wife I ever knew was Helen. She was beautiful and sophisticated and definitely didn't want to be called Grandma, so we called her "Aunt Helen." Their house in Crestline had a huge picture window, and as we turned into the driveway I could see the giant dining room table set for dinner. I wanted goldware just like Aunt Helen's when I grew up. They also had an amazing basement with a pool table and a bowling alley. I didn't think it could get much better than that.

My father's mother, Lydia, and her husband, Joe, ended up moving to Tampa, so visiting her was a weekly routine. My mother's mom and sisters continued to visit us every other summer or Christmas. My dad's sister came more often since her mother was here.

The family I grew up in was what I would come to reference as the "ideal composition": mom, dad, three children: Bonnie Lynn, Benjamin Lyle, and Becky Lee. I'm sure you see the pattern—BLC initials—which meant I had to be Becky and not Rebecca. I'm glad now that my name is Becky Burgue because I adore alliteration, however, as a child I always wanted to be Rebecca.

My sister was in many ways my inspiration. I followed in her footsteps to go to FSU and major in home economics education and return to Hillsborough County to teach. I distinctly remember the night of her wedding to her first husband being one of my saddest nights ever. Though I got to move into her room, I missed her so much. Attending the same schools after her, I was always compared to her, but that never annoyed me since we were both the same kind of student and both loved school. My brother was a different story—he didn't like school, he wasn't a good student, and hated being compared to us.

I now live in a new picture of "ideal composition": mom, dad, and two children, a girl and a boy. Pictures can't possibly portray the pain and the pleasures we've been through together, but we will continue, as long as life allows, to tell the story behind the pictures.

Perhaps you grew up in what you considered to be the ideal family or perhaps the family you grew up in was anything but ideal. Either way, we all have or had a dream of what our ideal family of the future will or would look like. How does your reality match up with that childhood dream? Each of these family memories I treasure had elements I would have liked to replicate, as well as some I loved to watch and wonder about but did not want to have play out in my own story. Have you taken the time to look at the pictures and share the story behind them with those you love? Those family stories deserve to be shared. We can learn valuable lessons from the lives of others. How will you choose to bring those stories into focus and pass them on?

Father, thank You for giving me the vision to see family members as people who are created in Your image. People who are just like me, fallible and fallen in need of grace and forgiveness. People who have learned from the situations of the past and made an effort to not repeat the same patterns of pain. Thank you for the design of families where we can live and love and learn that You have a perfect plan for each of us and those we love. I pray they will each come to know You and love You and realize their need for You. Thank you most of all for Jesus. Amen.

Chapter 10
My Life's Work

I always knew I would be a teacher. I loved school and I had the most amazing teachers at Cleveland Elementary School, who planted the seeds of a love for learning and teaching early in my life. Sligh Junior and Hillsborough High schools were also wonderful times for me, and my fondest memories involve the teachers who were willing to invest so much of their time and energy in my education and the pursuit of my dreams. Being able to go to just three schools and get to know the teachers and administrators there made it possible for me to have a consistent and secure feeling all through school.

I walked to all three schools and attended with the same neighbors and friends for twelve years. Graduating from Hillsborough High School in June 1970 with awards and scholarships was a proud moment in my family's life. I headed straight to Florida State University for summer session to get started on my goal of becoming a home economics teacher. I had a rough first semester, having never been away from home and now having freedom to do what I wanted when I wanted. My grades suffered but it was a wakeup call I didn't miss, and I got back on track toward my goal.

Graduating from FSU in December 1973 with a bachelor's degree in home economics education and a Florida teaching certificate, I started my life's work at my former junior high school, Sligh. I taught a life skills class to seventh graders for one semester, long enough to know they weren't interested in life skills, and that I wasn't going to spend my career teaching junior high students. My next assignment was at Tampa Bay Technical High School, where I spent the next four years teaching food service, clothing construction, family dynamics, and child development. There I learned that I wasn't teaching curriculum but rather I was teaching students.

As I reflect back on that now, those students' faces come flooding back to me. Faces like Danny, who was in my food service class and a proud member of what we called the Titan Terrace, a restaurant run by students for the faculty. Danny had an incredible smile and an amazing spirit and he went on to become an award-winning chef in the military. He is my friend today and has spoken on teach-in day at the elementary school where I volunteer.

Laura was in several of my classes and sought the direction and guidance for her own life that she wasn't getting at home. She still sends me a card every Mother's Day, and I attended her wedding and celebrated the birth of all four of her children. Many other students come to mind from those four years, and I treasure the memory of each of their stories.

Next, I went to MacDonald Training Center, where I had the privilege of teaching adults with developmental delays. The course was independent living skills, so I was getting them ready to live in their own apartments. These students were referred to as clients but they were so much more than that to me. When I reflect on the four years I spent with them, faces come to mind, like Linda, an exuberant young woman with Down syndrome. I attended Linda's funeral this past year and was reminded of her contagious zest for living. Then there was David, who at the time was a thirty-something man with cerebral palsy, literally a mind trapped in a body that wouldn't do what he wanted it to do.

David was an amazing man, and I learned more from him than he ever did from me. Twenty years later I had the privilege of sitting with his mother at his wedding, and we cried together, realizing that dreams you never had can come true. It was definitely one of those moments when you know that you know that you know why you teach! Years later I attended David's funeral. He lived to be sixty-six years of age, something the doctors never predicted. At his funeral, his sister read a poem he wrote while in my class—another moment affirming I chose the right life's work.

In 1984 I transferred to Gaither High School, where I spent twenty-six years teaching students in child development, family dynamics, early childhood education, life management skills, and clothing construction. The faces that come flooding back from these years include Tiffany, a turnaround student who went from unmotivated freshman to the "Outstanding Early Childhood Education" student who then graduated from USF with a degree in early childhood education and now has her own classroom, is a lead teacher, and is pursuing an advanced degree in administration.

Then was Brittany, who wrote in a note upon graduation:

You care about me, and you inspire me, teach me, and you believe in me. Your support has made all the difference in the path I ended up choosing. It's no wonder you are so highly respected; you have the perfect balance of professionalism and humbleness. My heart has taken on a new level of hope, and it is all because of you.

It just doesn't get any better than that!

There was Leanne: she soaked up all there was to learn and leaned on me as she experienced her parents' divorce and transitions through college. She became a home economics teacher, and I am thankful she was my student, then my colleague, and now my lifelong friend. I now have the privilege of watching her parent her adopted son and being a consistent part of their lives.

There was Jennifer: she was eager to receive everything I had to offer and she had a great gift for expressing her feelings on paper. She too had a difficult high school journey and to this day talks about the safety she felt in my classroom. Attending her wedding and teaching two of her three children and now being her lifelong friend are treasures I wouldn't trade.

There was Scott: a former principal and now a curriculum specialist, who wrote recently to say I am the reason he became an educator.

I also remember and treasure the faces of the preschool children I was privileged to teach over nineteen years in the Little Wrangler preschool at Gaither High:

- Dylan, who told his mom all he wanted for Christmas was a Miss Becky doll. Wow, that's humbling.
- Carson, who told his grandmother every day, "Miss Becky's the best!"
- Jacob, who was so excited to give me three quarters from his piggy bank for my birthday.
- Michelle, a three-year-old diagnosed with leukemia and her family, who clung to us throughout the process.
- Daniel, who got up to sing at the talent show and said, "Miss Becky Burgue, this one's for you" before he sang *Mr. Sun.*

The gift of teaching was one I received daily with humble gratitude. It was indeed a privilege in the highest sense of the word to be called to the profession of teaching. Teaching for thirty-six years, I had many memorable moments. Most people never experience moments like these, and I had them daily. I have had the joy of training new teachers and I always encouraged them to focus on the "best part." Not every day will be a best day, but every day will have a "best part." There is no greater privilege than to have been a daily, consistent part of a student's life and to know I have made a difference. I continue to make a difference in this repurposement (a word I created instead of that other re word many people in my life stage use) phase of my life as I teach adult childcare workers for the school system and also teach, train, and speak to women in Bible studies, retreats, and ministry leadership.

Where are you making a difference? Have you found the place you know you belong? Begin each day with a prayer that the Lord will show you who you are there for today. Believe me, God is faithful to answer that prayer. It is never too late to begin again. If you have a passion you know you want to pursue, start today. Others may discourage you from pursuing a path that doesn't have the monetary rewards other careers might, but the rewards are different and the satisfaction at the end of a day well invested is priceless. When you find the true path He has for you, it will never feel like work. I had an adult student tell me recently, "This seems like the perfect job for you!" Whew, that's a relief, since I've dedicated more than four decades of my life to this calling.

Father, You are the provider, the protector, and the giver of every good and perfect gift. May we always see our life's work as a gift from You. You are the One who designed me for a work that would bring You glory and honor. Thank you for the privilege of work. Continue to place people in my life that I can share You with. Continue to guide and direct each of us to the calling You have uniquely designed us for. Thank you most of all for Jesus. Amen.

Chapter 11
Collection and Recollection

Our journey to become a forever family began more than three decades ago. It has been a journey rich in milestone moments, from emotional first meetings to the mostly joyful, sometimes painful, process of coming of age for each of us.

My journey to write this collection of recollections began three years ago and it has also been a journey rich in milestone moments, from classes and practice to the sometimes-painful pursuit to get it all down, and finally the realization of why it was so important in the first place.

The desire to write the stories was birthed nearly two decades ago when my mom wrote hers. The determination to actually write my story came when my mom was diagnosed with Alzheimer's and I realized had she not written her story, it would have been lost forever. I would write mine, preserve the pictures, and reflect on the significance of the seemingly insignificant ordinary days to discover the possibilities each one held. I would leave a legacy of life and love in narrative while I could still retrieve the memories. The process has been fun, difficult, interesting, and therapeutic.

At my mother's homegoing service I was privileged to share the things my mother taught me:

- She taught me how to be a wife, mother, friend, and a Christian sister and mentor.
  - She was always there, cheering me on in all of my endeavors.
  - She taught me the value of lifelong friendship and I loved watching her enjoy her friends.
- She taught me how to cook and clean and iron and wash dishes.

Ground beef is the starting point of many great dishes, and that was before Hamburger Helper.

Whether cooking for the family or the entire elementary school, the most important ingredient is love.

We never had a dishwasher and I still don't have one.

Ironing was always my chore and I loved to sprinkle the clothes, roll them, put them in the refrigerator, and then iron them one by one.

- She taught me that love was in the details.
  - Always wear a slip.
  - Never put bottles on the table—use the relish dish.
  - Whether setting the table, painting a ceramic nativity, sewing a garment, or weaving a basket, the intricate details matter.
- She taught me how to celebrate all of life's moments and that meant rejoicing with those who rejoiced and weeping with those who wept.
- She taught me how to sew.
- She made all my clothes, costumes for school, and even my wedding dress.
- She taught me to be content in my circumstances.
- She taught me to stand up for myself and to speak up for others.
- She taught me to be patient with others and give people another chance.
- She taught me how to be a good daughter-in-law and a good mother-in-law. I loved watching her serve my grandmother, her mother-in-law.
- She taught me the value of the handwritten note.

I still have every note she ever wrote to me beginning with the notes on the back of the hospital menus when Ben was born. Since I wasn't allowed to visit, she would write me notes and wave at me from her hospital window.

Her letters when I was in college were often the only thing that kept me going, and sitting at the dining room table helping her with the Christmas cards was always a special time, and I still do this every year.

- She taught me to persevere through trials. And that came in handy during those last days of her life.
- She taught me to love God's Word and memorize it.

Through nightly family devotions and women's Bible studies—called circle meetings that were held monthly at our house—I loved watching her get ready for them as she got out the special dessert dishes and made root beer floats. I remember when I was finally invited to participate, and I haven't stopped those weekly studies.

- She taught me how to love children and how to teach them God's Word in Sunday school and vacation Bible school.

I have vivid memories of the children's sermons and then all the little ones leaving with my mom to go to the nursery. Because someone did that for her when she walked in with me in her arms when I was ten months old, she did that for other young mothers.

- She taught me to worship and to give God the glory in all situations.
- She taught me to sing the great hymns—all the verses!
- She taught me to be a lifelong learner, how to plan ahead, and to journal the journey.

The year she retired she took a class at USF in lifelong learning and wrote her own life story. What a gift that was to us; we are so thankful to have that now.

- She taught me to smile at others.

Her smile was a gift to all who knew her, and the greatest compliment I can receive is to be told I have her smile.

- She taught me the value of being part of a church family and what it really meant.

I remember watching her and my dad get ready for their Sunday school parties and I saw how they loved being with each other. My husband and I are blessed to enjoy that same kind of bond in our Bible fellowship class.

- She taught me how to grieve—not as one without hope but as one who has hope in the Lord that we will be with Him forever.
- She was just getting started teaching me how to let go.

I have my mom's story to remind me to use all that she taught, and now my children have my stories to remind them. I pray that my children will be able to say they learned to celebrate the journey, to savor the moments, and to give God the glory while learning to live a Philippians 4:11–13 life:

I have learned to be content whatever the circumstances. I know what it is to be in need and I know what it is to have plenty. I have learned the secret of being content in any and every situation whether well fed or hungry, whether living in plenty or in want. I can do all this through Him who gives me strength.

I hope they will always remember to:

- be strong in the Lord.
- not give up and to believe in hope.
- know that God has you, so don't be afraid.
- forgive others.
- remember the purpose for which God created you.
- always pray.

I hope they will be determined to preserve their pictures from the past and to pass them on.

What precious memories do you have that need to be preserved? Who needs to know how much they have taught you and influenced you along the journey? Will you start now to express these things in written and spoken word while there's still time? Will you live each day leaving a legacy for those who will follow, those you've been privileged to love and nurture along the way? Make a decision and a plan today to get started doing exactly that.

Father, You have placed us in families on purpose. You have given us the gift of others who have loved us well and nurtured, corrected, and cared for us so that we might become the people You have uniquely equipped us to be and do the work You have designed for us to do. You have also entrusted us with relationships where we can influence and teach the faith and values that were taught to us. Thank you for loving us more than we can possibly imagine. Thank you most of all for Jesus. Amen.

Part 2
Rescue

Verb: **rescue**; *past tense* **rescued**
res·cue / ˈreskyoo

> Save (someone) from a dangerous or distressing situation.
> *synonyms*: save, save from danger, save the life of, come to the aid of

- keep from being lost or abandoned; retrieve.
  synonyms: retrieve, recover, salvage, get back

A good story always has an element of rescue, that moment where someone is saved from danger. *Rescue* is an action verb, and action is required to take us out of a distressing situation and restore us to safety. My personal story doesn't have the elements of extreme distress, but we all have situations where we need to be rescued. I needed to be rescued from my own bad choices and from the consequences of my own destructive decisions.

I love the *retrieve, recover,* and *salvage* synonyms because they indicate there is hope for something good to come from something bad. It is possible for the mess I have made to be salvaged. I enjoy spending time in salvage yards and discovering items that have been cast away to uncover their repurpose value. I refer to myself as repurposed rather than the other commonly used *re* word for people in my age category. I have been rescued, saved, retrieved, and recovered for a purpose. I have been rescued from my own destructive patterns and from dangerous situations for a purpose much greater than I could have ever imagined.

Have you been rescued yet? Do you have thoughts, patterns, and situations, or perhaps even destructive relationships you need to be rescued from? Have you realized the purpose you were rescued for? As you read my stories, I hope you will reflect on your own stories of rescue and realize your worth in the eyes of the Lord.

In Your righteousness deliver me and rescue me;
Incline Your ear to me and save me.

Psalm 71:2, NASB

Chapter 12
The Sheltering Tree of Life: Branching and Blooming

The tree of life is an interesting visual metaphor. If you are a visual learner you probably find it much easier to grasp a concept with an image. The picture of a tree is something we can all relate to, and the seasonal changes a tree goes through parallel the changes experienced in our lives.

I have seen the tree from different vantage points throughout my life. A tree requires light, water, nutrients, and a strong and solid root system in good soil. I had a solid root system—provided by grandparents, parents, ancestors. I received water and light and nutrients in the form of love and enriching experiences.

Aside from these natural requirements for growth, trees also need pruning, a necessary and often painful process, to produce branching. The process of cutting off, cutting away, and cutting back all stimulate growth. I have a problem with this in my garden and in my life. I don't want to cut back or let go of anything even when I know I should and must.

My first branching experience was moving to Tampa in September 1953 at ten months of age. I don't remember, but I know it was major. My parents were both leaving their childhood homes and their emotional support system to start a new life in a new place with a new baby and a seven-year-old.

A new branch was grafted into the family tree in September 1958 with the birth of my brother, Benjamin Lyle Cheney. The addition of this new branch was a pruning experience for me. I was starting first grade and had to do it without my mother by my side because she was in the hospital. She returned home, but not alone; a new brother would certainly change the landscape I knew as home. The sheltering tree was expanding, and while somewhat painful emotionally for a young girl, I eventually learned to love my position as an older sister and a middle child.

More branching experiences happened when I entered school. The introduction of new people and new opportunities would have a profound effect on my tree of life. School and teachers who loved me and loved teaching planted the seed in me of a love for learning and teaching that would continue to grow and produce much fruit. Fruit is the product of a healthy, life-producing tree and also a visible sign that the tree is doing what is was designed to do.

Entering the world of work was a huge branching experience. My first job as a high school student in 1968 was at the W. T. Grants lunch counter at Northgate Shopping Center on Florida Avenue. This was a growth experience for me as I learned a new kind of responsibility. I listened to the advice of the other much older waitresses, who were quick to impress upon me how much they didn't want me to settle for this as my life's work. Sandi, Ethel, and Nancy were arborists of sorts, who made sure I would grow to my full potential.

College years and a marriage mistake were branches that shaped and sometimes threatened the silhouette of my sheltering tree. Bad choices and immature decisions cause knots on the branches and scarring on the bark that will forever be a part of the tree's character.

The death of my dad in 1974 felt like a barren period. There was pruning of relationships that were not promoting growth, and there was rain, lots of rain. No, really, lots of rain . . . it literally rained solid for two weeks after his death. I thought it would never end. It felt like the sun would never shine again, but it did and it does. The grief still comes, sometimes like a gentle breeze and other times like a gale force wind, but my tree of life still stands.

Remember that fruit I mentioned earlier? Well, a long and productive teaching career did prove fruitful and was a source of life and hope each day. I taught every age and stage from preschool to adult and developmentally delayed to gifted, and I found people are all much more alike than we are different. We all desire to be valued, loved, and acknowledged. We all want to know and be known. I am certain over my thirty-six-year career I learned more from them than they did from me, and I am so thankful. I had the opportunity to see the fruits of my efforts in the lives of the children I was allowed to love over all of those years. They went on to grow and prosper and use what they learned to enhance their own lives and the lives of others.

Another chance at marriage was like the season of springtime for the tree and continues to bring joy and contentment. New love and new life as a couple served to awaken areas that had seemed to be stunted from growth.

Three years into that new marriage, a life-threatening surgery—a total hysterectomy at the age of twenty-seven—was a literal and a symbolic cutting away of the diseased portions of my physical body and the prideful portions of my soul that resulted in total surrender to Christ and new life and real growth.

The blessing of two new branches on our family tree happened with the adoption of our daughter, Christina Lee, and then our son, Peter Richard. They represent fruit and all the possibilities it holds. Parenthood also brought with it the most painful pruning yet. For me, it was the realization that children aren't possessions to be held but people to be loved, and that God loved them first and He loves them more than I do. I knew that God had blessed us with children, and I trusted He would be faithful to see us through the growing pains of parenthood.

Many times it felt like our family tree's branches might break in the hurricane of a life-threatening eating disorder for Christina and navy deployments for Peter. I had to let go of my dreams for them and support them in the pursuit of their own dreams—a difficult and ongoing struggle for me.

The death of my mother-in -law, Zenaida, at age ninety-one, was a hard time for us all but it showed who the children had become—adults who knew how to grieve and how to comfort. They had become responsible, contributing, loving adults, so I guess those dreams I had for them really did come true.

My mom's diagnosis with Alzheimer's was another lesson for me about the storms and stresses on the tree of life and the tension between those things that have the potential to either strengthen or destroy the branches. And of course again I learned the realization of who is actually in control. I read every book I could get my hands on and researched all the current treatments, but this wasn't something I could fix. There seems to be a theme here of things I can't fix or control and trusting God with it all. My mom taught me so much, and in her last season, she taught me how to let go.

Retirement after more than three decades in a career where I honestly loved every minute and knew I was doing what I was called to do was a difficult and painful pruning process. I was privileged to be a daily and consistent part of the lives of so many students, and that is not easy to walk away from. Leaving my classroom on that last day to move into the uncharted territory of retirement was the cutting off of a branch that felt literally like the severing of a limb. I was blessed to have a life's work that brought such great joy and such sweet sorrow.

The death of my mom four months after my retirement was a pain I couldn't have predicted. I hope I will continue to age gracefully the way she demonstrated before my very eyes.

In this new season of transition I have found many opportunities for branching. Volunteering, serving, speaking and connecting in ways I never thought possible have all proved to be sources of new life and purpose that will continue to allow my tree to flourish.

Do you have a visual metaphor that helps you understand and relate to your life and the seasons you have experienced? Think about the changes and the growth and the lessons learned along the way. What are the lessons you have learned along the way and who or what were the unlikely teachers of those lessons? What are the constants that you have counted on during the seasons of change?

Father, You are the creative designer of the seasons, yet You never change. Give us Your eyes to appreciate the beauty and promise they all hold. You allow us to go through seasons of change and You have been with us through them all. Teach us to be mindful of the moments as we experience them and to appreciate the lessons learned along the way. You are faithful and we are thankful. Thank you most of all for Jesus. Amen.

Chapter 13
A Family Portrait: Christina's Story

I love children. I studied about children in college. I have taught children of every age and stage in the public school. I taught about children in child development, parenting skills, and family dynamics classes in high school home economics electives. I always assumed someday I would have children.

When I was in high school (1967–70), I imagined myself adopting children when I got older. Watching the army/navy training, white-knuckle birth films in Miss Lois Bray's child development class at Hillsborough High School made me sure I didn't want to take that route. While others were watching the film, I spent most of the time in the hallway with my head between my knees, trying not to pass out.

In the summer of 1976 I married Pete Burgue, and following a lakeside wedding, Hawaiian honeymoon, and the textbook-ideal three years of marriage before starting a family, we were ready for children. We soon realized being ready wasn't enough. Infertility due to endometriosis and a complete hysterectomy drastically changed the parenthood pathway for us.

We began the adoption process, working with Catholic Social Services and social worker Robert Disbennett. I am an advocate for all potential parents, biological or adoptive, going through the process we were required to complete. If the process to become parents was more carefully undertaken, perhaps parents would be more prepared, children would be planned for, and families would be strengthened from the start. Every child deserves to be welcomed by parents who are prepared for them and truly want to love them.

As a couple, we examined our reasons for wanting to be parents and evaluated the way we were parented. They looked at our family history and our financial history and interviewed our friends. They did an individual study, a couple's study, and a home study to determine if we would be suitable parents. In fact, we might not have central air and heat today if it hadn't been for the preparation we did for the home study!

We received a call from the agency saying they had a potential child for us but that she might have some problems. I was teaching at MacDonald Training Center at the time, and I remember sitting down in my office to take the call. I was anxiously ready to write all of the details on a legal pad on my desk. Two pages of notes later, outlining all the problems she might have, I made an appointment for us to go to the office to meet her.

We met our soon-to-be daughter at the Catholic Social Services on Bay to Bay Boulevard in Tampa, and I knew the moment we saw her we would be bringing her home. Pete wasn't quite as sure, since he is the cautiously optimistic type. I used all of my child development knowledge and training to do my own evaluation and decided that no matter what might be wrong, she deserved a chance and we could give her that. We only had the weekend to furnish a nursery, and with our modest income and limited budget, when we won $1,000 at the annual credit union meeting that weekend we saw God providing our answer.

February 25, 1981, we brought her home. Christina Lee Burgue looked like a little china doll in her pink-and-white dress and bonnet. We loved her immediately. Her black hair, dark eyes, and olive complexion were a beautiful combination; pictures didn't do her justice. Our prayers to become parents had been answered and a brand-new journey had begun. I am forever grateful to the birth parents who made the decision to give her life and to make it possible for her to have the best life possible with two parents who would love her unconditionally, forever and always.

She was seven months old at the time and had been with foster parents since birth. Our first night together as a family was a little rough. She cried, I cried, we rocked, and Pete wasn't quite sure what to do. A few days later she fell asleep with her hand on his chest, and the bonding had begun—she had captured her daddy's heart.

October 29,1981, at 10:15 a.m., with Judge Vernon W. Evans Jr. presiding, we testified to our love for Christina and promised to be the best parents we could be, and then we received the final decree of adoption. It was truly a day of celebration. We had become a family, and like the poem on her wall so poignantly stated, she hadn't grown under my heart but in it. Life would never be the same at Burgueworld.

What a huge understatement that became. Christina brought the extremes of joy unspeakable and grief unimaginable. There were the typical ups and downs of parenthood and also situations we never dreamed would happen. She was a child with an intensity like I'd never seen. In school, she was every teacher's ideal student. Her love language is gifts, and she loves to purchase and package the perfect gift. She was always a very spiritual child with a connection to God that made our nightly family devotions interesting. I remind her continually that God loved her first and loves her more. I remind her that He had His hand on her before she was born (Psalm 139) and that He has a perfect plan for her life, a plan to prosper her and not to harm her, a plan to give her hope and a future (Jeremiah 29:11).

Parenthood is the most extreme example of entering uncharted territory. We can read every book we can get our hands on and we recall our own childhood and how our parents parented, but we can never be completely prepared for the challenges ahead. I wouldn't change a thing because this is the path God planned for us, and I trust He will see it through to completion. I always thought the term adult children was a little strange, but now that I am the parent of two of them, I know this parenting journey is a lifetime one.

Becoming a mom, the process of parenthood, changes you from being the picture to being the frame. Where are you in the process? Are you still trying to be in the center of the picture or have you accepted your place in the supporting role?

If you are a parent, how has parenting changed you? What impact did your birth or adoption have on your family? How has the way you were parented influenced your parenting practices? Have you taken the time to reflect on that and to appreciate those things your parents did that you held on to and those you chose to leave behind? What parallels do you see between parenting, and being parented and God's love and provision?

Father, You are the One who formed us in our mother's womb. You have a perfect plan for each of our lives. You loved us first and You love us best. May we look to You for the example of how to best love each other. Remind us that our life is not our own but rather that we were bought with a price. Teach us to trust You completely through every trial and triumph of parenting and being parented. Thank you most of all for Jesus. Amen.

Chapter 14
Peter's Story

Sitting across from my thirty-two-year-old son in a Seminole Heights coffee shop on a rainy September afternoon, I asked and responded to probing and soul-searching questions. I remember an earlier, simpler time we he asked me from across the table, "Can you see that?" as he pointed above his head, making reference to the speech bubbles in cartoons and comics. I really wish I could have seen that then and I really wish I could see even more now.

The process of becoming a family is definitely a journey and not a destination. The day we brought Peter home was not at all like we had pictured. Leaving home that morning, we thought the feeling we both had in the pit of our stomachs was butterflies. Arriving at the building and riding up the elevator seemed like déjà-vu. Entering the office, there he was—this fair-skinned, curly-blond, green-eyed boy was our son—sitting on that same couch where we met our daughter two years earlier.

Altering all our plans of a show-and-tell tour on the way home, we went straight to Grandma Burgue's so she could meet Peter and then to Grandma Cheney's so she could meet him, but that's as far as we got. The butterflies turned into a full-fledged stomach virus. Our journey as a family of four began with a lot of help from the extended family, even having to spend the night at my mother's house. The last thing a young mother with a new child wants. The first night was rough—the days ahead would be better.

This fair-skinned little boy kept me on my knees as I prayed for wisdom to parent and love him well. I knew it would be a challenge when one morning I was awakened to his little voice calling out to me, "Mommy, Mommy, the dark has opened up." Who talks like that? Who thinks like that? The days ahead continued to show us that this was one bright little boy who saw the world through a completely different lens. His early school experiences were difficult as he had trouble relating to the other children. His kindergarten and first and second grade teachers enjoyed him and fostered his creativity. Then there was third grade! Let's just say it was not a pleasant year for any of us.

The high point of Peter's elementary years was his experience with the Young Astronauts Club and a second-grade teacher who truly understood and loved the challenge of teaching gifted children.

Peter, so smart and verbal, read everything he could get his hands on and had an uncanny ability to put together complex puzzles. Other children didn't "get" him and we knew he was exceptional. We didn't want him labeled but knew he needed strategies to learn to cope with these differences. His connection to music became his salvation in junior high and high school, with the discipline of the band director helping him order his world. Friday night football for me was all about the band at halftime.

Peter graduated, and because of his SAT scores was accepted to college and went for a year, though there is no evidence to support that. One day he came home and announced that he had joined the navy. We couldn't have been any prouder. His years in the navy behind him, he returned home and attended college classes and finally decided to move to Orlando to pursue his lifelong dream of working for Disney.

After many starts and stops and ups and downs he has achieved that dream. In the process, he met his wife who also loves and works for Disney. They are perfect for each other, as they share interests and dreams. She gets him and she provides the balance, love, and acceptance he has always longed for. Their wedding vows truly expressed the feelings they have for each other and the acceptance and appreciation they have for their differences and similarities. Many couples enter marriage with the idea that they will change the other person. Not these two—they expressed their thankfulness for each other's unique personalities and gifts in front of God and witnesses. I am so thankful God led them to each other. To hear his wife say on the day they became engaged, "This is the best day of my life," and know she is talking about your son's marriage proposal, is a feeling that is difficult to put into words.

The Mother's Day lunch when they asked if I would officiate their wedding was a moment I will never forget. Praying together and planning for their day was an amazing journey. It was a perfect day—weather, witnesses, and wedding vows sincerely spoken. What a privilege it was to officiate their wedding, and the connection that created is one I will treasure forever. Some friends traveled a long distance to celebrate with them, and some family members put aside longtime feuds to be there together. It was, as they say, a picture-perfect day and night. Everyone was genuinely happy for them.

December 3, 2016

I have learned from parenting Peter that it is okay to dream and that those dreams can become reality. I have learned to come alongside him and be supportive of his dreams rather than insisting on mine for him. He challenges me to read and watch and listen to things that stretch my intellect and broaden my horizons. He helps me see the world through his lens, one that looks beneath the surface and sees beyond the obvious. He has much to offer and so much to say; he has taught me to listen more than I talk and to accept rather than to judge. He is so smart and he would definitely be my "phone a friend" if I were ever on *Who Wants to Be a Millionaire.*

I miss our daily conversations when we rode to school together those high school years but I now look forward to the phone calls and intentional monthly face-to-face meetings when he just wants to run something by me or tell me something he's discovered or pose a clarifying question about the past. Those rainy-day, coffee-shop moments of soul-searching questions and probing possibilities form a mother-son relationship that is anything but stagnant. He is now a husband, and who knows, maybe someday a father, and I will keep on dreaming with him instead of dreaming for him.

What lessons have you learned from parenting or watching others parent or from being parented? We all fit into that scenario of being parented, and we either want to emulate our parents or go the exact opposite direction. Parenting adult children is a supportive role. It is now hands off and prayer on as we encourage them to realize their own dreams and as we hope they will share them with us. Do you have those moments of memorable conversations or contemplative silence that frame your relationships with your own parents or with your children? Are you celebrating the journey, realizing how fast the time has gone? Begin today to view the world through someone else's lens and learn to picture the possibilities.

Father, You are perfect in all of Your ways, and You have a perfect plan for each of us. Thank you for the opportunities You provide for us to grow and learn and see things from a new perspective. Give us grace to love and forgive those who have hurt us along the way, our parents and our children. Thank you for giving us grace and forgiveness for the times we have failed to love them the way You love us. Give us eyes to see and ears to hear the hearts of those You allow us to love. Thank you most of all for Jesus. Amen.

Chapter 15
When Does a Timeline Become a Love Line?

Peter's second grade assignment: create a timeline of your life. Seemed harmless enough, but I was certain Peter's teacher had no idea of the angst this created in the heart of an adoptive mom. *How secure is Peter in his identity?* I wondered. *How does he feel about sharing it with his classmates?* I would find out soon enough.

When I picked up Peter and Christina from afterschool care, our afternoon routine began. Peter asked his usual questions: "Did you make any money today? Is there enough for a snack?" I smiled and answered, "Yes and yes," as we pulled into the Circle K. Snacks eaten, when we arrived at Burgueworld, book bags were thrown on the floor by the dining room table, awaiting my random daily check. Peter headed straight to the fridge for a drink while Christina turned on the TV to watch *Little House on the Prairie.*

My book-bag inspections began with Christina. Her work was neat and in order, check complete. I turned to pick up Peter's bulging bag and rummaged through the wrinkled papers. Wait, what's this rolled up like a scroll? Unrolling it I read, The Timeline of my Life by Peter Burgue, written in his distinctive handwriting with colorful doodles. I ran my finger along the squiggled timeline, smoothing the paper as I went: August 8, 1982—I was born. March 7, 1983—I was adopted. August 1987—I went to Disneyworld. He had it! I breathed a prayer of grateful joy and my heart smiled.

It's a milestone moment that reminds me of this mysterious, magical process of becoming a "forever family." There are so many unknowns in this parenting journey and especially in the adoption journey. Many fears, often unspoken, lurk in the back of your mind about how you are doing. At times, like Peter's timeline assignment, the fears surface and you must face the tough questions about biological parents and heredity versus environment. Our daughter was never one to ask those questions and she got nervous when our son did. He would spew the line, "You're not my mother" when he thought it would push the emotional buttons and take the heat off of his behavior. I needed to know he was secure in his identity as our son. It is true that most of our fears never become reality. He indeed was secure in the family and he saw his adoption as a natural part of his timeline. That day, reading his second-grade timeline, I realized that a simple plotting of chronological events on a horizontal rendering had become a love line.

This process of becoming a family started for us in February 1981, the day we met our daughter. All the papers we filed, home studies we endured, interviews we attended separately and together . . . none of it could have prepared us for that day. Arriving in separate cars from our respective work places, Pete and I met in the parking lot, rode the elevator up and stopped at the edge of the office. Looking at each other, we took a deep breath and opened the door. She was sitting on the couch without any assistance. This seven-month-old baby girl with a little round face, dark hair and olive complexion—the same as Pete—magnetic eyes, and cherub smile drew us in. Mr. Disbennett left us alone with her. I lifted her into my arms and began walking around the room with her. I wore a dress with a flower print and a gold locket around my neck. Her chubby little fingers immediately grabbed the heart-shaped locket with a grip that wouldn't let go. That wasn't the only heart she captured. That day we met our daughter; in a week we took her home.

A meeting on a calendar, a plot point on a timeline, but a heart connection forever.

March 1984, now a family of four, we got up extra early. Pete took the day off, and we headed downtown for another milestone moment, Peter's final adoption. Our son read all of the stop signs and pointed to all the flags and red lights along the way, telling us when to stop and go. We arrived at our attorney Mr. Flanagan's office and walked with him to the courthouse. Peter, in his little brown-and-white suit and striped socks, squirmed in my arms.

When we arrived at the courthouse and made our way to the chambers of Judge Vincent Giglio, a fifteen-minute formality of questions and answers began. Mr. Flanagan asked our name and our intention to adopt, and we stated our son's name, Peter Richard Burgue. We then awkwardly posed with Judge Giglio behind his desk for a family photo. It was silent for a moment and then a conversation not on the docket happened. Judge Giglio turned to Christina, and Mr. Flanagan pointed to her newly adopted brother and asked, "Do you know who this is?" She responded with a big smile and answered, "He's Peter. He's happy and so are we!"

Another meeting on the calendar, point plotted on a timeline, heart connection communicated, love line expanded.

Many years later the journey of highs and lows was recorded in photos, albums, and journals, but mostly pondered in the heart of an adoptive mom. The love line is strong and the celebration continues.

You probably also have your moments and milestones and all the highs and lows plotted on a timeline on paper or in your mind's eye. Reflect on those milestone moments and think about the people and situations that brought you to the present. Have you allowed yourself to really process them and put them in order to see the impact of the timing? While your memories and moments are different, they too are growing into love lines. If you have memories too painful to plot or timelines that seem to never turn to love lines, give yourself permission to create new ones of your own.

Father, thank you for the memories and moments in our lives that cause us to realize what's important. Give us new insight to put those small snapshots in order and see the bigger picture. Give us glimpses of Your glory in the ordinary times of our lives. Thank you for the timeline of Your love, which gives us hope each day. Thank you most of all for Jesus. Amen.

Chapter 16
One Phone Call

One phone call can change a life forever. It may be a notification of a great blessing or deliver a devastating blow. I'm sure we've all experienced those calls that when received, stopped us in our tracks, and everyone around us knew by our silence and the change in our demeanor that something major was happening.

The first of these calls I remember was in my childhood home when a call came in from Ohio to tell us my grandfather had died. I remember the somber, serious look on my father's face and the silence after he hung up that was so different from anything I had ever experienced. The call was followed by quiet conversations between my parents, making plans for how to manage the next few days, which would require a trip to Ohio for my dad.

A similar call was received a few years later to notify my mom that her mother had died, but this seemed different; no less important, just different. Between those two calls came another call that devastated us all. Working for the City of Tampa Recreation Department in the summer of 1974, I received a call at work that would forever change and alter life as I knew it. The call was to tell me my dad had suffered a massive heart attack while delivering a speech at a downtown hotel. They called me because they knew I was working for the city and they couldn't reach my mom. One moment I was lining up children for a summer swim lesson, and the next I was rushing to my father's side, not knowing what I would find when I arrived. I found that my father had died. I wouldn't use a phone call to notify anyone else—this information had to be delivered personally.

A phone call received in February 1981 brought the good news that a baby girl was available for adoption into our family. A phone call two years later in March 1983 brought the news of a baby boy who would come home with us. Those two phone calls made us parents. All the phone calls after that were tests of parenting.

Anytime the phone rings after a certain hour of the night can create an anxiety that is hard to describe but certainly manifests itself in the physical symptoms of a racing heart and feeling of suffocation. We have had our share of those calls as parents. Calls in times of crisis and calls of cries for help have recently been replaced by calls for comfort and counsel—a welcome change.

One of these life-changing phone calls was from the nursing home on October 17, 2010, to say that my mom had died. I knew it was coming, but the phone call finalized the impending feeling of dread. They say you feel like an orphan when you lose both of your parents, and it seems the person making that phone call doesn't really understand the impact of their message. As I write this, it has now been seven years, and I still miss my mom every day and have the urge to call and share exciting news or seek her wise counsel.

I never liked talking on the phone; I much prefer face-to-face interaction. For me all the new technology in the world will never take the place of the warmth of a smile or the comfort of a heartfelt hug.

Each of these phone calls represented a paradigm shift in my world, a turning point when everything changed. I have moments when I realize and reflect on the changes that are taking place in my life. I don't like change. I am a person of routine and consistency, and when that is disrupted by unexpected detours it can be unsettling. It is especially those times that cause me to return to the One who doesn't change, the One who never leaves or forsakes. I make the choice—and yes, it is a choice—to trust God with the unknown. The journey metaphor that has always been my motto is more important than ever during these times of uncertainty. It is a reminder to celebrate every step of the journey, especially those I couldn't have possibly planned or prepared for. Those phone calls present us all with the opportunity to make a choice to trust God with the future and to wait expectantly for the treasures He has in store in the midst of our trials.

What calls have changed the course of your life? What calls have you had to make that would alter life for the person on the receiving end? What method of communication do you prefer for receiving important news? That call could come anytime. In the meantime, we must celebrate the journey and enjoy the moments while we can. How will you resolve today to make precious memories with the time you have been given?

Father, You have given us the gift of today—a day we will never get back and a day we can spend living and loving. Help us to be responsive to Your prompting to express our feelings to one another while there's still time. Cause us to be intentional when it comes to scheduling time first with You and then with one another. Teach us to gratefully count the blessings and live every moment to the fullest, realizing they are each a gift from You. Thank you most of all for the gift of Jesus. Amen.

Chapter 17
Patriotic and Parental Pride

I have always been a proud American. I loved to recite the Pledge of Allegiance in school, and I always wear red, white, and blue on the Fourth of July, Memorial Day, and my birthday (Veteran's Day). Election day was always one of my favorite days, and going to vote with Mom and Dad was a real treat, especially when my dad's name was on the ballot. I must confess that I even clean house to patriotic music. But never has there been a day that I experienced more patriotic pride and parental pride at the same time than that day in May 2006 when my husband and I rode in with the crew on the USS Nassau as they returned from a six-month deployment. This is known in the navy as a Tiger Cruise.

Considering the sequence of events of the past few years of our lives, I was extremely proud when our son, Peter, came home and told us he had decided to join the navy. With each new accomplishment, we could see our son overcoming his lifelong challenges of feeling "less than" and of quitting just before his goal was reached. Each of his graduations from the navy's boot camp and power school were proud moments of personal victory that far surpassed what we could have imagined, and they will remain in my memory forever, but the twenty-four hours of our Tiger Cruise on May 3–4, 2006, simply cannot be topped.

The invitation arrived and we immediately accepted. I couldn't imagine any parent turning down this chance of a lifetime. In the past only dads had been invited to participate in the Tiger Cruise, so I was thankful that moms and even children were now included. We made all of the arrangements to arrive in Norfolk, Virginia, on May 2 and be rested for the 4:30 a.m. bus ride on May 3 to Radio Island, where we would meet the transport landing craft.

Boarding the landing craft was thrilling to me, in spite of my tendency to get seasick. I wore my antinausea bracelet, and did observe another mom throwing up in the corner, but I determined not to let anything ruin this experience for me. I truly would celebrate every moment of this journey.

With choppy seas and salt air in my face, I remember catching a glimpse of his ship—the USS *Nassau*, an amphibious assault ship—in the distance and my excitement and anticipation continued to build.

Our landing craft drove right into the ship—*inside the ship*—an incredible experience. As we disembarked, observing all the young men and women in their work blues there to greet us, I was overwhelmed with a sense of gratitude for their service and sacrifice. Then the mom in me took over as I saw my son's smile. I felt a sense of relief at seeing him safe after a six-month separation, and a joy unspeakable as I swelled with parental and patriotic pride all at the same time. Hugs and kisses and tears were shared all around this massive ship, and then the show-and-tell began.

Peter couldn't wait to show us everything about his floating home with all the same excitement and joy he had as a small boy when he would show us his classroom or summer campground. He took us to his work station, his sleeping quarters, and of course the dining hall. Peter was an E3 master mechanic and had his own area that he explained to us fully. Many valves and gauges had to be set with precision. I didn't understand any of it, but it all certainly sounded important and vital to the total operation. He introduced us to his commanding officers and those under his supervision, and all had good things to say about my son. That is always an encouragement to a mother's heart. Peter was anxious for me to try on the diving gear, a heavy tank strapped to my back and a mask strapped to my head that I had to breathe through, and while I was a little apprehensive, I wanted to get the full experience. He was patient, helpful, and reassuring, and I enjoyed the moment of realization that the proverbial "tables" had certainly turned. The cautionary warnings—"Be careful. Lower your head. Walk slowly. Tuck in your wings"—were now coming from him and not me. Well, actually, I've never said, "Tuck in your wings." That was a new one for me.

Two highlights while on board were the refueling process and the flight demonstrations. I was amazed and impressed with the precision and care taken with every detail. Still, the best was yet to come. Thursday morning, May 4, the crew paraded in full dress whites around the outer edge of the ship for the official welcome home. I was not prepared for how this would feel.

At the port, people were gathered as far as the eye could see to welcome these sailors home. My patriotism was at an all-time high to actually witness this homecoming firsthand. Add to that my son being one of those sailors, and the pride exceeded any measurement. All the fears of the unknown that go with having a son or daughter serving our country were gone as we rode safely to shore. All the reasons Peter gave for why he knew he needed to enlist flooded back and were affirmed as I stood behind him and as he stood at attention on the edge of the ship. Truly it was a moment to celebrate the journey and to breathe a prayer of thanksgiving.

Have you had fearful times that turned to times of immense pride and satisfaction? I'm sure you have. Perhaps you are still in the fearful time, holding your breath, waiting for the moment when you can finally relax and realize it was all worth it. There is a time to be thankful for both of these experiences, because one makes us appreciate and recognize the other. Think of times someone told you they were proud of you. Now think of someone who may be waiting to hear that you are proud of them.

Pride is a word with two meanings. It can be destructive when it is focused on ourselves in comparison to someone else, and we are cautioned against it. Then there is the pride we feel when a task is completed, the satisfaction in a job well done. If you have experienced that kind of pride, take the time to reflect on it and, if needed, express it to the person you are proud of. I guarantee they will be happy to hear what you have to say.

Father, You are our tower of refuge and strength. You are our protector and defender, our hiding place, an ever present help in times of trouble. You allow us to experience all kinds of feelings and emotions. We ask You to help us process and express our feelings first to You and then to each other. Help us to keep our pride in check. Give us courage to express our pride to others You have placed in our lives. Help us to glorify You in all of our feelings, thoughts, and actions. Thank you most of all for Jesus. Amen.

Chapter 18
Pictures of Pain and Pleasure

I have never been one to count the days but rather to make the days count. When I look back at the days I have been blessed to live, some stand out in vivid color. They are the extremes on the spectrum—the high and the lows. All of the "ordinary" days are developed by the lessons learned on the mountaintops and in the valleys.

The sudden and untimely death of my father in June 1974, when he was fifty-two and I was twenty-one, will always remain in my memory with vivid detail. I was working for the City of Tampa Recreation Department at the time. The children were lining up for swimming lessons when I was called to the phone. I was told my father, who was the acting mayor of Tampa at the time, was speaking at the Floridian Hotel when he had a heart attack, and I should come right away. I went to the hotel and rode with him in the ambulance to the hospital, but they were never able to revive him. I had to let the rest of the family know, including my mother.

It was summer so my mother and sister were both in workshops, but I finally reached them to tell them to come to the hospital. My brother, fifteen at the time, was working at the auto repair shop in our neighborhood. My father's mother, Lydia, confined to a wheelchair, was sitting in her kitchen listening to the radio, as was her custom. I'll never forget the sound of my mother's screams when she learned that her husband, the love of her life since she was a teenager, had died.

I then rode in a police car from the hospital to tell my grandmother the news, praying I would get there before she heard it on the radio. My brother did hear the news on the radio of a car he was repairing. He got up and just began to walk. We didn't find him until later that day. The selection of a casket and planning of a funeral all had to be done, tasks we are never fully prepared to do.

Learning to live life without the one who had been the steady, consistent rock of the family was and continues to be a difficult process. Grief comes in waves and we must learn to ride them. My father's death was a deep personal sorrow, however, the resulting victory was that the events during that period of grief gave me the courage to leave a marriage that had been a mistake in the first place.

Another contrast of personal sorrow and personal victory is when I found out at age twenty-seven that surgery to remove a tumor would result in a hysterectomy and the inability to have biological children. This was a deep and personal grief, but the victory came. First, in the realization that a decision to give my heart to Jesus at age twelve was real but limited, and second, that I had always held on to a portion of control and frequently tried to manipulate circumstances and bargain with God. That all ended the summer of 1980 after my surgery, when I released that control and totally surrendered my life to Christ. There is truly, as the old hymn says, "Victory in Jesus." "I have come that they might have life and have it to the full" (John 10:10).

Our daughter, Christina, was born in July 1980; that timing was no coincidence—exactly nine months after my hysterectomy. We adopted her in February 1981. The adoption process is a beautiful picture of God's love for us. He adopted me, and I am an heir to His kingdom, a daughter of the King.

Our son, Peter, was born in August 1982 and adopted into our family in March 1983. He had a hole in his heart, and while physical illness is always a season of personal grief, again victory came. We spent a lot of time with doctors and tests and much time in prayer. One day, in the heart specialist's office, when our son was all hooked up like ET so we could see the picture of his heart, the doctor said, "The hole was there, but now I don't see it." Christina, at three years of age and with all the faith of a child, said, "Dr. Brodsky, I told you, Jesus filled the hole in Peter's heart." Another beautiful picture of God's love for us.

The next contrast of sorrow and victory came when our daughter was twelve. I taught high school students child development and parenting skills, family dynamics, and early childhood education, where I was able to talk about how to really love your family and give children a sense of acceptance and belonging. Yet my own daughter was about to enter a dark time in her young life when she began to struggle with a life-threatening eating disorder.

I had taught about nutrition and wellness as well as the lack of healthy habits and the recognition of eating disorders, but now my home and family was shaken to the core. My husband and I had lived in the same house (still do), had the same phone number (still do), and worked for the same people all of our married life. What had seemed to be a safe, predictable, controlled family life was now anything but. This was only the beginning of five years of struggle and questions I continually asked God and myself.

This was the child who told the children on the bus that we were going to "dopt" a baby. When they asked her, "What's dopt?" and she said, "My mom doesn't have the parts it takes to make a baby," all of the children looked at me as if I should have a big hole somewhere. Now I was questioning if I had the parts it takes to be a mom. Yet God was teaching me that this wasn't a competition and I didn't need all of the answers. I just needed to love her. Scripture says He is sufficient for all of my needs, and I just needed to trust Him and to let Him know the desires of my heart.

God loved us and her through it, and today she is a beautiful young woman who still struggles when stressed but who knows and has experienced the unconditional love of God. That love provides the acceptance and acknowledgment, the value and recognition we all desire. Again, the victory was in Jesus and the abundant life He alone provides.

The sorrow of that season of sickness and struggle was rewarded in a personal career victory. In the fall of 1996 I was selected by the faculty at Gaither High School to be the Teacher of the Year. This was a humbling experience, as I was the first vocational teacher ever selected, and I also believed my colleagues to be the best teachers I had ever known. For them to select me was an amazing honor and privilege, the high point of my professional life.

It didn't stop there though. After the written application process, I was selected as one of eight finalists for the Hillsborough County Teacher of the Year. I was interviewed by the "power brokers" in our county and was so excited to have an audience with them to be able to tell them why I loved what I did every day in the classroom, and to share my teacher's heart with them—and they listened. When I left that interview I was walking several feet above the ground. A few weeks later on February 15, 1996, at a lavish banquet surrounded by the greatest educators in the county, I was announced as the 1996–97 Hillsborough County Teacher of the Year. For a year I was the ambassador for education in and from Hillsborough County. It was an experience I will always treasure, and the best part was the congratulatory notes, cards, and letters that came from colleagues and students and parents of students. Victory is not the trophy or prizes won but rather the hearts that are touched and the lives that are changed along the way.

We have experienced many more moments of pain and pleasure since then. There was a beautiful wedding of our daughter with a ceremony that honored God and participants who had been my students and were now precious friends. Then the pain in the realization that the two making the vows weren't best suited for each other and a divorce barely a year later was a painful process and a reminder of my own past mistakes. Pleasure came in observing the personal growth and maturity that results from picking up the pieces and moving forward.

Being that support person and sideline cheerleader for adult children can be a painful role. Knowing when to speak and when to be quiet is a constant struggle. The pleasure often comes in the moments when I appreciate my own parents and the fact that they never gave up on me in spite of all the pain I know I put them through. There will undoubtedly be more pain to come in this process of aging. I want to handle it all with grace and with much prayer and thanksgiving for the opportunities I've had to persevere and the pleasures I've been privileged to experience.

I am living a victorious, abundant life, yet I know there will be more sorrows and victories ahead. I agree with Paul in his letter to the Philippians when he wrote, "I have learned to be content whatever the circumstances. I know what it is to be in need, and I know what it is to have plenty. I have learned the secret of being content in any and every situation, whether well fed or hungry, whether living in plenty or in want. I can do everything through Him who gives me strength" (Philippians 4:11–13).

What pictures of pain and pleasure do you have or have you had in your life? Have you learned to see the painful times as opportunities to grow and learn? Perseverance comes through trials, and in many situations, if we really open our eyes and hearts, we can see the triumph even in the midst of the trial. A daily prayer I ask is, "What do you want me to learn from this?" instead of praying for God to fix this or even to fix them—the people in my life. I am sure we learn more in the painful, difficult times than we do in times of pleasure and plenty. Take the time to think about the lessons you've learned in those tough times and give thanks for who you are today because of those painful times.

Father, You grant me life in a family and community. You are the giver of grace and mercy and strength for the daily trials I face. You sent Your Son to experience life as a man, and He faced all the same pain and pleasure I face. Let me look to Him for the example of how to handle each day with prayer and a closer walk with You. I trust You with all our tomorrows and all the pain and pleasure they will hold. Teach me to walk in your way. Thank you most of all for Jesus. Amen.

The Tampa Tribune, Friday, February 16, 1996

Burgue is teacher of the year

By B.C. MANION
Tribune Staff Writer

TODD L. CHAPPEL/Tribune photo
Becky Burgue accepts her award, with Superintendent Walter Sickles, left, and Ed Shaw of Caspers Co. & McDonald's Restaurants watching.

TAMPA — As soon as Superintendent Walter Sickles uttered the words "preschool program," supporters of Becky Burgue — Hillsborough County's teacher of the year — began screaming and applauding.

"Now, wait a minute. We have to let everybody else here know," Sickles urged — quieting the cheering section so he could pronounce Burgue as Hillsborough's 1996-97 teacher of the year.

"Her classroom motto is 'Celebrate the journey, don't wait for the destination,'" Sickles said. "Tonight, we'll celebrate this outstanding educator."

"I'm overwhelmed," said Burgue, who teaches child-care classes and runs a preschool program at Gaither High. "When I heard him say my motto, that's really true. I have enjoyed every step of this journey, from the time I decided to become a teacher until this very moment, and I know I will continue to enjoy that journey."

She recited a song that her preschoolers sing. It goes like this: "It's my job, and I like it fine. No one has a better job than mine."

"That's exactly how I feel," Burgue told the audience of about 1,000 at the Thursday night banquet in the Hyatt Regency Tampa ballroom.

She was selected from a group of eight finalists who emerged from the district's 161 top teachers in their schools.

Leanne Vaughan, a former student of Burgue's, said the teacher changed her life.

"I knew that something was different about her as soon as I walked into her classroom," said Vaughan, now a teacher at Middleton Middle School.

Burgue offers unconditional love, Vaughan said.

"She's the reason I'm a teacher. I was going to be an astronaut. I changed my mind and set my sights a little higher," Vaughan said.

BECKY CHENEY BURGUE

Becky Burgue was flying high when she was announced as the 1996-97 Hillsborough County Teacher of the Year. She was even more surprised to learn that she would soon be jumping out of a plane because of it.

Florida Metro

Monday, February 10, 1997

■ Dan Ruth takes on leadership ... Column, Page 4

Not your typical school dropouts

SUMMARY: Hillsborough School Superintendent Earl Lennard and "Teacher of the Year" Becky Burgue show teacher-administration unity.

By ACE ATKINS
of The Tampa Tribune

TONY HATHAWAY/for the Tribune

Becky Burgue and instructor Mike Hoogsteden, above, head for a happy landing. Burgue persuaded schools chief Earl Lennard, right, to join in

> " I've always encouraged my students to take risks ... and face their fears. "
>
> **Becky Burgue**
> Hillsborough "Teacher of the Year"

ZEPHYRHILLS — When the 13,500-foot jump was canceled Saturday, a smile of relief passed the lips of Earl Lennard, superintendent of schools. But Sunday morning when the cloud-covered skies opened into a view reminiscent of a religious postcard, everyone at Skydive City knew it was time.

Lennard was asked to dive by Hillsborough "Teacher of the Year" Becky Burgue. When Burgue was honored last year, she won two skydiving certificates and later asked Lennard to join her. Neither the Gaither High School teacher nor the county superintendent had jumped before. But both wanted to take the plunge before Feb. 19 when a new "Teacher of the Year" will be named.

"At first my family was very skeptical of my sanity," Lennard said. "After Becky asked me to jump, I went through a careful thought process. I accepted the challenge to highlight the importance of teachers and administrators working together."

Burgue never considered herself a thrillseeker before Sunday's skydive. "I've never liked to ride the fast rides at the fair," Burgue said. "I guess really the teaching I do every day is a risk personally — you really have to open up and challenge yourself. People laughed when I told them what I was about to do, but I'm really excited."

Lennard and Burgue waited all Saturday afternoon for clearance. Friends and family looked skyward at Generation Xers plummeting to the ground in Birkenstocks.

Skydive City is a place where the tie-dyed listen to Hendrix and Marley over the PA system. Some jump instructors live in converted school buses topped with television antennas and flapping windsocks.

See JUMPERS, Page 8

JUMPERS/Educators take flying leap

◄ From Page 1

"I've always encouraged my students to take risks with their fears and face their fears," Burgue said. "After 22 years teaching I'm more enthusiastic now than when I first started."

Burgue teaches family and consumer science at Gaither.

Former student Louise Vaughn agreed. "Her enthusiasm is so contagious," she said. She chaperones her students to learn.

On Sunday, Lennard looked more relaxed than the previous day. He spent Saturday adjusting his belt, crossing and uncrossing his arms with a nervous smile on his

face. On jump day he left for an hour and pieds at home and much grey sweats with gold sweater emblem.

Burgue looked less relaxed on Sunday. Her speech continued as her tandem jump partner, Mike Hoogsteden, strapped the harnesses around her shoulders.

Hoogsteden explained, "We'll jump out at 13,500 feet and fall about 120 miles per hour. At 5,000 feet I'll open the chute."

Burgue said, "I trust my teacher."

Decked out in sunny jump suits, Lennard and Burgue followed their instructors to whom they were assigned during the skydivers to the tarmac.

plane "City Express." Two quaint-looking planes loaded into the sun, waiting "Right Stuff"-style across the tarmac. Lennard gave a shaky thumbs up.

Minutes later the plane climbed and soon both were appeared indistinguishable. The speck of Lennard and Burgue grew larger as their families waited breathlessly for a speck of parachute color.

The multicolored parachutes opened, and the 5-minute sail began. Fifty feet away the panicked arm of showing the sun appeared, and both headed smoothly.

Burgue and Lennard hugged, and Lennard said, "To the students of Hillsborough County — the sky is the limit."

Bay Crest Park · Carrollwood · Carrollwood Village · Citrus Park · Country Way · Dana Shores · Keystone · Lutz · Northdale · Odessa · Town 'N Country · Westchase

THE TAMPA TRIBUNE

Northwest

Wednesday, February 21, 1996

Teacher of the year accorded full red carpet treatment

Gaither High teacher is the first vocational education instructor to attain the county honor.

By B.C. Manion
Tribune Staff Writer

TAMPA — Becky Burgue walked under a canopy of swords and stepped onto a red carpet to welcome Tuesday morning at Gaither High School.

The teacher was returning to her first day of classes since being named last week as Hillsborough County's teacher of the year. She is the first vocational teacher to win the countywide honor.

Well-wishers eagerly waited, holding flowers and balloons, as a limousine approached the school at 16200 N. Dale Mabry Highway.

Jennifer Nusenbach, one of Burgue's former students, was among the people waiting. "I love every class she has had in other from 1988 to 1987.

"Anyone who's known her has just had a ray of sunshine wrapped around them," she said.

Gaither Principal Ken Adam said Burgue has a knack for making people feel welcome. She also imparts her love of teaching upon the students she instructs in her child care classes, he said.

"Each one of these kids hear warmth now for kids because of her," Adam said.

Pupils, faculty and friends greet Becky Burgue, teacher of the year, Tuesday morning at school.

Burgue teaches child care and runs a preschool program at Gaither.

She began teaching in 1974 at Northwood Training Center before arriving at Gaither when it opened in 1984.

CANDACE C. MUNDY/Tribune photo

Becky L. Burgue

Personal: Burgue, 43, is a daughter of Mary Cheney and H.L. "Doc" Cheney. Her father, who died in 1974 ...

Students call teacher a 'special friend'

■ From Page 1

Her approach has won many admirers.

"She teaches you what you need to know about life. She's not just a teacher, she's a friend," said Jiedi Butler, 18.

"She actually gets down and does stuff with us, what other ...

School welcomes teacher

■ From Page 1

because of her," Adam said.

Burgue teaches child care and runs a preschool program at Gaither.

She began teaching in 1974 at Sligh Junior High. Next, she taught at Tampa Bay Technical School and MacDonald Training Center before arriving at Gaither when it opened in 1984.

Her goal was to follow in the footsteps of her sister, Bonnie Stover, an award-winning teacher who launched the first day care program for children of district employees.

Stover, a teacher at Brewster Technical Center, also owns a limousine service. She decided to surprise her sister by subbing for the limo company that was supposed to pick up Burgue.

She said she'll give her sister a limousine ride to Orlando, if Burgue makes it to the final round of the state teacher of the year competition. The winner is announced in May.

Stover isn't the only family member proud of Burgue's accomplishments.

Burgue's husband, Pete, and their children, 15-year-old Christina and 13-year-old Peter, think she richly deserves the accolades.

"She's a really special lady," said Christina, a Gaither student.

"She was born that way," added Peter, who attends Ben Hill Junior High.

Jerry Skora, choral director at Gaither, was Burgue's teacher when she attended Hillsborough High.

"She hasn't changed. To me, she's exactly the same. She's a very positive person. She turned out to be a great teacher," Skora said.

Burgue said she loves her job. Students say she takes the time to find out what they have to offer.

That goes along with Burgue's teaching philosophy, according to her application for the award. Many of my students have been labeled 'unreachable' by others. "When they enter my classroom, I remove all the labels and begin to find out what is inside," Burgue

Becky L. Burgue

Personal:
Burgue, 43, is daughter of Mary Cheney and R.L. "Dick" Cheney. Her father, who died in 1974 while interim mayor of Tampa, was filling the unexpired term of Dick Greco, who had left the post to go to work for Edward J. DeBartolo Corp., a mall development company from Youngstown, Ohio.

She is married to Pete Burgue and they have two children, Christina, 15, who attends Gaither High, and Peter, 13, who attends Ben Hill Junior High.

Teaching experience:
Sligh Junior High, 1974; Tampa Bay Technical School, 1975-79; MacDonald Training Center, 1979-84; Gaither High, 1984-present.

State competition:
Burgue now competes for Florida's top teaching award, to be announced in May. Hillsborough's winner has been among the state's five finalists for four years in a row. Gaither teacher Jerry Murray won the statewide honor three years ago.

> ❝ She teaches you what you need to know about life. She's not only a teacher, she's a friend. ❞
> — Heidi Butler, 18

wrote.

Her approach has won many admirers.

"She teaches you what you need to know about life. She's not only a teacher, she's a friend," said Heidi Butler, 18.

"She actually gets down and does stuff with us, when other teachers would give us a worksheet," said Tracey Martinetto, 18.

"On the first day of school, I don't think anybody in homeroom 1816 realized what an amazing teacher and special friend we'd found," one student wrote on a greeting card signed by her homeroom class.

A former student popped by Burgue's classroom to drop off a card.

"Congratulations on becoming the Hillsborough County teacher of the year," the student wrote. "I knew that you could do it. You should be the teacher of all time. If there was a teacher's hall of fame, you would be one of my first choices."

CANDACE C. MUNDY/Tribune photo
Hillsborough County teacher of the year Becky Burgue works with Darren and Erin Domarecki in her classroom Tuesday morning.

Teacher of the year gets royal welcome

By B.C. MANION
Tribune Staff Writer

TAMPA — Becky Burgue walked under a canopy of swords and stepped onto a red carpet in a royal welcome Tuesday morning at Gaither High School.

The teacher was returning to her first day of classes since being named last week as Hillsborough County's teacher of the year. She is the first vocational teacher to win the countywide honor.

Well-wishers eagerly waited, holding flowers and balloons, as a limousine approached the school at 16200 N. Dale Mabry Highway.

Jennifer Nusekabel, one of Burgue's former students, was among the supporters. "I took every class she had to offer from 1984 to 1987.

"Anyone who's known her has just had a ray of sunshine wrapped around their heart that will warm them for a lifetime."

Gaither Principal Ken Adam said Burgue has a knack for making people feel at ease. She also imparts her love of teaching upon the students she instructs in her child care classes, he said.

"Each one of those kids has a warmth now for kids

See SCHOOL, Page 6

Chapter 19
I Don't Know How I Ended Up Here

"I don't know how I ended up here" could be said of many of my life's moments, and I imagine many of yours as well. Time passes quickly and sometimes we wake to find ourselves facing circumstances we never dreamed possible—some good and some not so good, but all brimming with possibilities and lessons for the journey.

"I don't know how I ended up here." There have been a lot of times and places that prompted this response in my life:

- a college dorm room with a roommate who clearly didn't know how to make a bed or do laundry
- an aisle leading to an altar where a horribly mismatched matrimony was about to take place—actually there were a couple of those
- a high school classroom full of students who weren't much younger than me waiting to see what I had to say
- a first night home with a crying baby and two fledgling, first-time parents having a rocking-chair moment

- a ballroom filled with family, friends, colleagues, and more responding with resounding applause to an announcement of an accolade never imagined
- a small plane at 13,500 feet with an open space that a tandem partner and I crawled toward and thrust ourselves through
- a high school auditorium with a capacity crowd watching my child on stage
- three separate scenes standing by coffins much too soon, shoulder to shoulder, with children who had suddenly become adults
- a gathering of folks thirty-six years in the making, wishing to reflect on the journey and celebrate the possibilities of the next phase
- the waiting room of the social security office, entertaining a small child with how many things we could create from a purse strap as I anticipated the proverbial payoff for a life of dedicated work
- a beautiful bride approaching to take the hand of my son as I prepared to make the act official
- a hospital emergency room and a husband in severe pain
- a waiting room with an eerie silence, imagining the worst
- a sibling and spouse road trip with me as the driver and two siblings snoring in stereo in the back seat
- opening the mailbox to find an AARP magazine addressed to me!
- passing the mirror quickly and doing a double take as I catch a glimpse of my mom looking back at me

I don't know exactly how I ended up here—many times—but I know the One who does know. I am thankful for a life of faith that is firm but fluid, and I look forward to the continued flow.

Think of the situations and circumstances in your life that have brought you to this present point. Attempt to capture those moments in a simple sentence that best describes those times and trials. As we reflect on our lives, we see moments that were quite unexpected, and also those that arrived due to our own choices. We live in community with others, so the decisions we make affect not only us but everyone we love, and their decisions affect us. Think of those moments and those decisions, whether good or bad, and take a moment to be thankful for the possibilities and opportunities each one held.

Father, You are the author and finisher of my faith. You are not surprised by any of the situations I've found myself in. I want to walk in Your way and be aware of Your will in my life. Make me more aware of Your presence and more obedient to Your will. I want to learn the lessons You are teaching me in each situation and circumstance. Thank you most of all for Jesus. Amen

Chapter 20
Snapshots So Far and Those Never Taken

As I've mentioned, my motto has always been "Celebrate the journey; don't wait for the destination." Yet I'm not sure a timeline of my life would always illustrate that I have consistently lived out that motto.

As I've previously shared, I was born in Galion, Ohio, on November 11, 1952, and moved to Tampa when I was ten months old, so my life in Florida is all I know. I was blessed with parents who loved me and one another well. I am the middle child of three. We lived in the same house all of my childhood and I attended only three schools: Grover Cleveland Elementary, Sligh Junior High School, and Hillsborough High School, all within walking distance of my home. I lived a consistent, comfortable life filled with people I knew I could count on. That's cause for celebration.

My parents valued education and spiritual nurturing and taught me to do the same. The entire family doing church together every Sunday was a memorable celebration on my journey. I loved school and my teachers, with one exception. My third grade teacher was having a bad year, and therefore so were the twenty-five children in her charge. I spent the majority of that year in the hallway for talking, whistling, or other celebratory behavior. In junior high I discovered FHA, the Future Homemakers of America, in my first home economics class. I was hooked and I continued through high school. I became a state officer and set a goal to become a home economics teacher so I could be an FHA advisor and give students what was given to me—the opportunity to develop leadership skills. I headed to FSU in the summer of 1970 to, as the FHA creed says, make that dream become a reality.

A snapshot not taken at that point on my timeline is the one after a gynecologist told me—at age nineteen, in college, and unmarried—that I should get pregnant because it would help my physical condition. I shudder to think how following that advice would have altered the pages in my life's album and I am glad that photo was never taken.

I had a failed marriage at age twenty, mostly due to immaturity and poor judgment, and while that wasn't much of a celebration, it was a learning experience. Right before I would head to Ft. Lauderdale for my internship, I married the wrong person at the wrong time in an attempt to make my wrong choices seem right. The night of the rehearsal dinner, my father, who was my human hero, reached over and whispered in my ear, "Look around. Are you sure you want to do this?" The fact was, I did not want to do that, and I knew it wasn't the right thing to do, but I did it anyway. A beautiful wedding and beautiful pictures that I wish weren't in my album.

Another snapshot not taken during this part of my timeline is the one of my then home management housemate—now lifelong friend—Christy and I going on an interning adventure to Ft. Lauderdale. We would have interned together in high school and junior high home economics classes and lived the single life, enjoying a new kind of independence. Instead I went with my new husband, who would six months later be my ex-husband. I do often wonder what those snapshots would have looked like and how the next pages of my photo album would have been altered if only Christy and I had gone together.

December 1973, at age twenty-one, after three years and six months, with a degree in hand, I returned to Tampa to teach home economics at Sligh Junior High, the place where my dream began.

The journey and the celebration continued with the right new marriage and parenthood. After a 1976 lakeside wedding in the spot that became our home, and a Hawaiian honeymoon, we began the journey toward parenthood. Infertility due to endometriosis and a complete hysterectomy caused our journey to take a different turn. For a fleeting moment, I thought about the advice that doctor had given me when I was nineteen and wondered if I should have taken that advice; then I might have a child. It was definitely only a fleeting moment. We began to pursue adoption. In February 1981 we were blessed with a beautiful baby girl and then again in March 1983 our son came home. Our family was complete but the journey had only begun.

Have you ever wanted to turn back time and do things differently? Better yet, have you realized how grateful you are that you couldn't do that?

As the career portion of my journey continued, I taught at three schools for a grand total of thirty-six years before retiring in 2010 with quite a celebration. My parting words of wisdom to my colleagues:

As I leave to enter uncharted territory I wanted to leave you, my colleagues at Gaither High School, some parting thoughts:

May you continually monitor your teacher's HEART!
When asked what you teach, may your response always be, "I teach students."
May you always remember you have a great privilege and a great responsibility.
Remember to:

Hear their hearts
Encourage them
Appreciate them
Reassure them
Treasure the time

May your teacher's heart be enlarged as you continue to "Celebrate the journey"!
You will remain in my thoughts and prayers.
I am forever grateful for the time we have shared.

I share these words on this page because one snapshot I've never taken is the one where I *always* shared my heart and words that I knew I should share; at times, for one reason or another, I didn't. I am glad I have grown to be more obedient to the promptings to share and the vulnerability to care, even when it's risky.

Snapshots not taken during these years of my timeline all involved sharing of the heart and savoring the moments. I am happy to say there aren't too many not taken and that volumes of albums are filled with the ones that were.

So here's my advice to you as you read this entry: be sure your camera is always charged and your heart is always full, and in the words of the infamous Dr. Seuss, *"So... be your name Buxbaum or Bixby or Bray or Mordecai Ali Van Allen O'Shea, you're off to great places! Today is your day! Your mountain is waiting. So . . . get on your way!"*[1] And remember to take lots of pictures.

Do you have a song waiting to be sung?
Some art waiting to be hung?
A piece waiting to be played?
A scene waiting to be staged?
A tale waiting to be told?
A book waiting to be sold?
A rhyme waiting to be read?
A speech waiting to be said?
A road waiting to be taken?

If you do, don't wait any longer. Figure out what is holding you back. Is it fear that stands in your way? Perhaps other things that seem more urgent get your attention and you make that infamous promise to "Do that tomorrow," and tomorrow never comes. Instead of living with regrets over the pictures not taken, picture the path you want to pursue, and take the risks to follow that path. You'll have many treasured memories from your life's journey and many actual snapshots rather than imagined ones or regret over the ones not taken.

> *I will sing of the LORD's great love forever;*
> *with my mouth I will make your faithfulness*
> *known through all generations.*
> Psalm 89:1

Father, You have protected us from decisions that had the potential to be destructive. You have provided wisdom and discernment even when we didn't have the sense to seek it. Thank you for unanswered prayer. You have provided a way of escape when it seemed there was no way. You have directed us in the way we should go. Your plan and Your path are always the best. Teach us to be good listeners and followers. Thank you most of all for Jesus. Amen.

Part 3
Renewal

noun: **renewal**
re·new·al / rəˈn(y)ooəl

> The replacing or repair of something that is worn
> out, run-down, or broken.
> *synonyms*: renovation, restoration, modernization,
> reconditioning, overhauling, redevelopment,
> rebuilding, reconstruction

Renewal is the process of a brand-new start. The first two
sections have brought us to this final section of taking
something and replacing it with something better. New and
improved. I love the synonyms of *renovation, reconditioning,*
and *reconstruction.* I think of the reconditioning crème I rub
on leather furniture to give it new life, or better yet, a
clearer look at the character produced by age. The
opportunity to begin again, afresh and anew. The Bible says
God's mercies are new every morning, so we have that
chance for renewal each day. I choose to look at each new
opportunity I'm given as a chance for renewal for myself
and others.

In what situations have you needed to hit the restart button? Each season has a purpose on the calendar and in our lives. Spring is evidence that the winter has done its work. If we are patient in the cold and barren seasons of life, they will be followed by new growth and new beginnings.

This section on renewal is evidence that there is new life and new hope available. It is encouragement that those dreams we never had can come true. Do you need encouragement today? Do you long to begin again? Are you ready to bring the broken pieces and allow God to rebuild something beautiful? It is possible to breathe new life into every relationship and to recognize that we have each been rescued for a purpose. Your story and mine are not finished yet.

Therefore, if anyone is in Christ, he is a new creation; old things have passed away; behold, all things have become new.
2 Corinthians 5:17, NKJV

Chapter 21
My Favorite Daily Delights

One of my favorite verses of scripture is Psalm 37:4, "Delight yourself also in the LORD, and He shall give you the desires of your heart."

The word *delight* makes me smile. It is one of those words that sounds like it feels. Delight results from engaging in activity or thoughts that bring joy, and I love the feeling I get when I experience it in the context of my everyday, ordinary life. A grand event is not required to encounter delight.

A top ten list of my daily (or at least with frequent regularity) delights would have to include:

- 2:00 p.m. lattes
- knick-knacks given to me by precious people throughout the years
- quiet prayer time with my Bible on the porch overlooking the lake
- road trips with Pete—especially to the *Country Living* Fair in Stone Mountain, Georgia, each October when Country Living magazine comes alive
- handwritten letters

- sunflowers, bananas, and yellow roses
- singing the great hymns—all the verses
- snuggling with the dogs

browsing antique stores and looking through old pictures
teaching, speaking, and sharing my testimony

Of all my favorite delights, celebrating special milestone moments is my most favorite. I believe we all can find moments to celebrate every day, but the "special" occasions bring smiles and warmth to our spirit when we remember. Looking through scrapbooks and old photo albums at the snapshots of these celebration moments brings back the sights, sounds, smells, and all the sensations that made that moment a memory.

Swimming with the dolphins
September 2009

Family picture, 1981
Standing (l-r): Joe Schulte, Pete, me and Christina, Bonnie
Stover, Mary Cheney. Seated (l-r): Lydia Schulte, Shawnee Amber,
and Ben Cheney

I want to spend my days doing things that matter for eternity, which is why my favorite things aren't really things at all but the people and the purpose behind the memories. When I tell people I enjoy dusting, they think I'm crazy, but for me dusting is a trip down memory lane as I clean the knick-knacks and treasures given to me through the years by my children, students, and friends. Each one takes me back to the time and the celebration moment that special treasure was so carefully selected to commemorate. They are all displayed in places of prominence in my home. I enjoy looking at them and being surrounded by the love they represent.

I keep handwritten letters and notes in large hatboxes throughout the house where I can just reach in and pull one out to read. I'm immediately taken back to that place in time when the letter was written. I have all the love letters my mom and dad wrote to each other and all the letters they both wrote to me when I was in college. I have every note Pete has written me throughout our dating and marriage, and the letters my children wrote from camp. I have cards and notes my adult children sent me, and now notes of thanks from our precious daughter-in-love. Communication methods have changed, and I have changed with them to stay connected. I will text and use messenger, however, I still prefer a handwritten note, a carefully selected card, an actual phone call, or best of all, a face-to-face visit. We have chosen to be intentional about seeing our family in person at least once a month and we meet halfway to make that happen.

I treasure the time spent with my husband and children, realizing that days are short and we should make the most of every minute. I don't want to waste time on petty things that only rob me of today's joy. Hundreds of songs have been written about missing the moments that matter. Obviously many people fall into the trap of not seeing what's right around them every day. I don't want to do that. I will delight in the firsts, the lasts, and all that lies in between. I will continue to be aware of my favorite things and take the time to enjoy them every day, thankful that God's mercies "are new every morning" (Lamentations 3:23).

The word *delight* means "to be changed by the light." What brings you delight? One of the best things we can do when we are feeling down or discouraged is to make a conscious choice to do something that brings us delight. Prayer and praise are my first choice, and that time spent with the Father prepares me for spending time with family and friends. Take an inventory of the things that delight you and give yourself permission to do them with regularity. Treasure hunt each day for the delightful surprises God has for you and write them down. This creates a brain connection that cannot be broken. Each morning brings a new day for new delightful opportunities!

Father, Your mercies are new every morning and Your Word brings delight to my heart. Remind us to be mindful of the delightful surprises You send for us to enjoy. Give us grateful hearts as we take inventory of each day. Replace our disappointment, discouragement, and depression with delight. We make a choice to step into Your light and allow it to change and renew us. Thank you most of all for Jesus. Amen.

Chapter 22
Universal Dreams

The dream of becoming a wife and mother may be nearly universal to little girls. The path that leads to that dream becoming a reality is anything but universal.

As a child, I played with dolls, dressing and undressing them, rocking and feeding them, all a rehearsal of sorts for what was to come. My brother was born when I was seven and I spent a lot of time practicing on him. "First comes love and then comes marriage and then comes Becky with a baby carriage"—childhood rhymes made it sound so easy. As a teen, I took home economics and Red Cross babysitting classes and joined Future Homemakers of America, increasing my skills as a future wife and mother. I was exposed to the FHA creed then, and those lines still ring in my head today:

We face the future with warm courage and high hope. . . .
For we are the builders of homes,
homes for America's future,
homes where living will be the expression of everything that
is good and fair,

homes where truth and love and security and faith will be realities, not dreams.

The creed continues to be recited to this day with some minor changes, but the original will always resonate in my heart.

As a high school student, I continued my home economics classes, taking courses in child growth and development and family living, and I was elected to leadership positions in Future Homemakers of America on the local and state levels. All these accomplishments more than qualified me for a wife and mother position, I believed.

I vividly remember the child development class with Miss Lois Bray at Hillsborough High School. (Wait a minute: she wasn't married and she had no children.) I sat in flickering shadows with the clicking of the 35mm projector as we watched the birthing scenes in the army/navy training films she showed in class—at least up to the white-knuckle, screaming-mother, crowning-baby part. At that moment I had to escape to the hallway and sit with my head between my knees. I decided then this childbirth thing wouldn't have to be the way I would become a mom. I would adopt. This would only be a slight alteration of the original dream.

As a college student my quest to learn all I could about child growth and development became more than just preparation for parenthood; it would be my life's work. I would later teach home economics and specialize in children and families. Before graduation, I married—a developmentally appropriate, poor decision. I was still on the path to my dream in spite of all I had learned about family dynamics: dating, engagement, marriage, and—just like the family dynamics textbooks—the last chapter of that marriage, divorce. This was not only a painful experience and admission of a wrong choice but another detour in the path of my wife-and-mother dream becoming reality.

As a divorced, rookie teacher of child development and family dynamics, a second chance at love and marriage was on my horizon, and I was back on my dream path.

Infertility and a hysterectomy altered the path to parenthood again, and it seemed that harsh reality would replace my idealized dream. Reality is difficult to accept and this certainly wasn't something I would have chosen. Would I never be a mom? Was all that preparation wasted? Would I have been able to get pregnant in that first marriage? Did I miss my chance? This pity party lasted a short time until I was jolted back to reality with the thought of the declaration I had made to myself in that high school hallway.

My reality became God's possibility. He reminded me of my statement as a high school student about adoption. A new path, a new dream, a new opportunity to become a mom. Pete and I applied and prayed and prepared. Again, nothing universal about this process. The preparation involved applications, interviews, and home studies. And waiting—for us, ten months of waiting.

God is faithful. We finally got the call and met our daughter. With a weekend to prepare, we won a $1,000 prize at the annual credit union meeting—more affirmation of God's favor and faithfulness. Our dream was indeed becoming a reality, even though the path to get there was not what I had envisioned. God was literally giving new life to our dream.

The first night at home with our daughter, she cried, I cried, and Pete wondered what we had done. The next morning we couldn't imagine life without her. The cards and gifts and baby showers often happen after the child arrives with adoption. Friends and family celebrated with us and we were now a "forever family" who would celebrate "special days" and fill out an adoption book instead of the universal baby book that spends the first twenty pages on the pregnancy and birth. Adoption has its own special language and not-so-universal challenges.

A call came two years later asking if we were interested in adopting a baby boy. We didn't pursue this or reapply as we had done the first time, so being God-fearing, Spirit-led people, we figured this was divine intervention and we said yes. The day we picked up our son, the proverbial butterflies in my stomach turned out to be full-blown flu. Granted, we were new at this but there was no parental provision for the flu bug on our first day with our second child.

The universal parenting questions like "Where do babies come from?" and "Is Santa really real?" pale in comparison to the not-so-universal questions of adoption, like our daughter's question, "What's dopt?" to which I explained the what and why. Then there was our preschool son's question: "Did I have a tail when I was inside the mom who gave me life?" Along with the question came the realization that even at his young age he truly got it.

We didn't become parents in the universal way but we are no less parents, now and forever. A home with *truth, love, security,* and *faith* is indeed a reality, a dream come true.

Do you have dreams that seem to have taken a detour? Is there something you long for that you think might never become a reality?

The universal truth that parenting gets harder as children get older is also true for adoptive parenting. Both of our children are now just a little older than we were when we brought them home. Both of them still crave that assurance of an unconditional love that doesn't give up. We have been through our daughter's two failed marriages and our son's multiple job losses and we won't give up. The questions get harder and the consequences more devastating.

They are both much more like us than they want to admit. Our daughter looks like her daddy and our son looks like me. Challenging for my husband, they both act like me. They both have a keen sense of right and wrong and both know and have experienced the unconditional love of a forever family. We have always had a healthy appreciation for the fact that they both came to us with a biological blueprint for life that we had nothing to do with, but we provided them with a nurturing environment that also had a profound effect on who they continue to become. A beautiful combination.

From this side of life, I wonder what I might say to my childhood idealistic self with the initial dream, or my high school idealistic self with the "I can change the world" attitude, or my college disillusioned self who'd just divorced. What words of wisdom might I have to offer? I would say, "Celebrate the journey and enjoy the twists and turns you didn't see coming, because that's where the real adventure lives." I would say, "Talk to God about everything and trust Him with the results." I would say, "Document the journey so you will clearly see God's hand every step of the way." I would say, "Take chances, be spontaneous, share your heart, and open your home." I would say, "Don't take yourself so seriously; laugh at yourself and love freely."

What would you say if you could counsel your younger self, knowing what you know now? How do you see your dreams from this side of life? Will you take your own advice starting right now?

What truths are universal? I truly believe we are all much more alike than we are different. We all desire the same things. We all have the same desire in our hearts to make our dreams come true. So here are some other universal truths I've learned along the way:

- Dreams do become reality.
- Every experience from the past prepares us for the future.
- Detours can take us in a different and better direction.
- Forever begins with a moment and never ends.

Treasure the moments and take the time to reflect on the dreams that have become realities in a different and probably much better way than you could have imagined.

Father, You have placed eternity in our hearts. Your plans for us are far better than anything we could have asked or imagined. Thank you for all the ways You have directed our paths and prepared our hearts along the way. Cause us to wait expectantly for what You have in store each day. Thank you most of all for Jesus. Amen.

Chapter 23
A Story of the Heart

A beautiful Sunday spring morning just after sunrise.

Standing on the sidelines, I cheered on the runners who approached the last mile marker with the end in sight. I smiled as I heard a child shout, "Don't quit on me now, Dad." Anticipating my thirty-something son rounding the corner, my future daughter-in-law was on the fence with her phone positioned to capture the first glimpse of the man she loves completing his second half marathon. This was all too much for a mom's heart to take in at once.

Like a slideshow on an automatic timer set way too fast, the images appeared in my heart and mind:

- getting on an elevator as a couple with our not quite three-year-old daughter and getting back on the elevator a few minutes later, a family of four with our new seven-month-old son
- a "not so sure about this" sister meeting her brother for the first time
- at the office of the heart specialist as he says, "Peter's special need is physical; he has a hole in his heart."

- the heart specialist's office a few months, when the doctor tells us, "I know it was there, but now I don't see it," and Christina, with all the faith of a child, explaining to him that Jesus had filled the hole in Peter's heart
- a boy and his dog sitting back-to-back on the living room floor
- a young astronaut field trip with his dad
- a first-chair saxophonist at the middle school holiday concert
- Friday night football games and watching him perform in the precision of the marching band
- a soloist at Showcase Finale singing, "You have given me life" from the song "I Am Found in You."
- a hug good-bye as he leaves the safety and security of home to join the navy during war
- riding on the transport to his ship as our seaman returns from deployment
- standing in the shadow of our navy seaman in dress whites at attention
- gathering pictures of Christmases past for centerpieces for their upcoming December wedding reception

Life's moments recorded like blips on the screen of an echocardiogram—the rhythm of a mother's heart.

The sound of Jen's voice interrupted my memories as she said, "Here he comes now," bringing me back to the present. There he was, arms held high with a smile of satisfaction at the completion of another goal.

More milestone moments were on their way—a wedding and all the possibilities that holds, daily challenges faced, and dreams becoming realities. This is the son who faced multiple challenges in his three decades of life: a forceps birth that left a scar on his forehead, a diagnosis of a hole in his heart, numerous challenges in the early years of school—from being awkward and not fitting in, to cruel bullying on the bus and at school.

At times I believed my dreams for my son might never come true, dreams of work and love and friends and fulfillment that every mother has. Let me encourage you to never give up on those dreams for your children, and let me remind you that even dreams you never had can come true. Let me just breathe a prayer of thanksgiving for God's faithfulness through it all as I celebrate and recall this one.

What are your dreams and desires for yourself and your loved ones that you have never dared to share? Will you let God renew your hope and refuel or reroute your dreams? Take the time to reflect on a moment when you were able to observe a dream become a reality in a way you could have never imagined.

Father, You are the one who gives us our desires and dreams. Allow us to feel Your presence in each milestone moment. Give us dreams that are bigger than anything we can imagine. Cause us to remember Your faithfulness through every step of the journey. Thank you most of all for Jesus. Amen.

Chapter 24
Snapshots So Far and Those Never Taken

As I wrote personal notes and addressed our Christmas cards one Thanksgiving night, a long-standing family tradition, I was suddenly struck by a sobering thought. With the addresses in front of me, I saw more deletions than additions, so many names crossed out because they are no longer with us. I'd sat a table every Thanksgiving since I was a child, carefully addressing cards. Now, decades later, the reality of how much had changed hit me.

The change was not only evident in my address book. Decorating the day after Thanksgiving is also a long-standing tradition. There was a time when I decorated my own house, my classroom, three other houses, as well as my daughter's salon. Now I decorate my own house, the salon, and two cemetery plots. I never complained about decorating at my mom's or my mother-in-law's or my grandfather's mobile home and then his room at the nursing home. The progression of decorating with and for my mom went from her house (the one I called home as a child) to her mobile home to her studio apartment. The Lord took her home in October 2010, so I was spared decorating in the Alzheimer's unit room. I always took the time to pay attention to detail. I have inherited the decorations from those who are no longer with us, and I treasure the memories as I painstakingly position them in special places.

My mom's hand-painted nativity scenes—one for upstairs and one for the entry way—her ceramic Christmas trees and snowmen so lovingly detailed, the antique snowman who now stands on my piano where old familiar carols are played and sung. Then there are the special ornaments: olive wood that Joe brought to me from Israel, photo ornaments of the grandchildren that I gave my mom every year, her "poppin' fresh doughboy" ornaments, and the handcrafted ornaments Christina gave me each year. Then there is the beautiful Christmon tree that now stands in my loft with its white-and-gold ornaments made by my mom and the women of the church. I will never forget how beautiful that tree was in the front of the sanctuary in the church of my childhood.

The seasons have come and gone quickly over my six decades of life. The cards and carols continue, and I find myself reflecting on the consistency of the Christmas message in the midst of changing circumstances. I realize we aren't losing anything. The past is part of us and we take it with us as we move into the future. There is consistency in change. Moments and memories carry us through. As you experience change and transition, focus on what has remained the same. What has carried you and will continue to carry you through? Who is the One who never changes? Who is the One who will never disappoint?

Jesus remains the same yesterday, today, tomorrow, and forever. And He is still the centerpiece of my celebration each Christmas season and forevermore.

A year later and change was still a constant. Thanksgiving dinner was still the same but the faces around the table changed from last year. I still wrote out and sent Christmas cards, but I couldn't find the cards on Thanksgiving night, so a couple of days later I ended up driving them to Christmas, Florida, to mail them, creating a brand-new memory. The decorating still began the day after Thanksgiving but seemed to drag on for days.

I do love the decorations but dread taking it all down and the bare look of January. Instead of thinking of January as bleak or bare, I choose to think of it as a brand-new start—a blank page in my journal and a clean slate with all kinds of possibilities. I am compelled and captivated by what the Lord is showing me as possibilities for a new year, so I will keep that thought in front of me as I seek His consistency in the midst of constant change.

Our lives are a beautiful picture of the past, present, and future blending together to create a new image. Our memories are the connecting pieces joining these together. Change is constant, we can count on that, and through it all Christ is consistent. We can count on Him.

Take a moment to ponder the seasons of change in your life and the elements that have been consistent in the midst of those changes. Chose to focus on those elements and look forward to the possibilities they present.

Father, You are the kinsman redeemer. You are our provision and our source of all that is good and perfect. You are the constant source of love and grace in the midst of change that can be daunting and difficult. You are faithful though it all, and for that and so much more we are thankful. Thank you most of all for Jesus. Amen.

Chapter 25
The Lost Art of Letter Writing

I love to receive a handwritten letter in the mail. It all started as a child when my Aunt Dorothy would write from Columbus, Ohio. I was seven years old and I absolutely idolized my aunt. She had what sounded like an exciting life. Her letters always included the details of what was happening in her life, and then she would ask me about mine—which meant she expected a reply. My mom taught me to respond to the questions in any letter I received as I answered, and she taught me to write the date I answered on the envelope. And so my practice of letter writing began.

The highlight of every Christmas season from as far back as I can remember was the ritual on Thanksgiving night when my mom and I would sit down to write our Christmas cards with an individual handwritten note in each one. Though my mom is no longer with me, I continue this tradition today. I love hearing from people how much the handwritten notes are anticipated and appreciated.

I have scrapbooks filled with handwritten cards and letters received throughout my childhood. When I left for college, I took note cards, envelopes, and stamps given to me by my high school home economics teacher (a great idea by the way) so I could keep in touch. After graduation, one of my college friends moved to California, and for forty years we never called or emailed, we just wrote letters. I still have every one of them.

So while the handwritten note is not a lost art for me, it is for our world today. A Newsweek article written in January 2009 gives us some insight into the situation:

> *The letters people left behind are invaluable evidence of how life was once lived. We know what our ancestors ate, how they dressed, what they dreamed about love and what they thought about warfare, all from their letters. When we reflect on how dearly we would cherish letters written by people in bondage or any people who, through some circumstances of history, were voiceless, we begin to grasp the preciousness of the written record—any written record; laundry lists, ancestral records in family Bibles, love notes—and how poorly historians of the future will be served by this generation, which generate almost no mail at all. There is a multitude of digital information today but the problem is there is not enough information about what we think or how we live. When we read a letter, we develop an image of the letter writer unavailable to us in any other way. Writing a lot of letters will not turn you into Lincoln or Shakespeare but if you do it enough, you begin to put your essential self on paper whether you mean to or not. No other form of communication yet invented seems to encourage or support that revelatory intimacy.[2]*

A friend shared with me recently the joy of her holiday baking day as she used a recipe in her mom's handwriting. Just the sight of that writing took her back to the smell of the kitchen and the memories of time spent together baking. Can you relate? Do you have memories of special handwritten notes? We have lost something precious by not continuing the art of writing. I wonder if you sense this loss as I do.

131

So think of a letter that is meaningful to you- Take a few minutes to remember some of the details of that letter.

Without knowing anything in particular about each of the letters you thought about, here's what I do know. The person who wrote the letter was:

- someone who cared about you enough to write a personal note.
- someone who took time to write.
- someone who knew your name and where you live.
- someone who bought a stamp and properly mailed the letter.
- someone who planned so you would receive it in a timely fashion.

Before you even opened the letter, so much had already been communicated.

Though I don't know you personally, here's what I do know about you:

- You were thrilled when you opened the mailbox to find real mail.
- Seeing the handwriting flooded you with emotion.
- Some of you opened it immediately at the mailbox.
- Some of you took it to a special spot in your home and sat down to savor every word from the precious opening and closing terms of endearment.

So, was I right?

Being a teacher, I know there is an important brain component involved in the writing exercise. Something about the brain-to-hand connection simply doesn't happen with texting, emailing, or typing. Putting pen to paper makes us better readers and writers and we process what we write more deeply. Students are better off with a composition pad than an iPad. Putting pen to paper encourages pause for thought.

The lost art of letter writing can be rediscovered. We can revive it here today. Find a piece of stationary or a blank note card and write the name of someone special on the envelope, someone who will be the recipient of your handwritten note. Now take your note card and open it up, write today's date, write your salutation, then begin your special message. Your message can be anything personal: where you are, what you had to eat, how you are feeling, and how you feel about the person you're writing.

Don't let it stop there. Look up the person's address, purchase a stamp, and send off your note with a blessing.

You could start a trend if you send the recipient a box of note cards and a supply of stamps to keep the tradition going. Write on, precious friends.

Father, You designed us for community, and community requires communication. We are so thankful You desire a relationship with us. We are so thankful we can communicate with You through prayer. Give us Your words to share with the people in our lives. Help us write words of encouragement that bring life. Thank you for Your Word of truth and life and thank you most of all for Jesus. Amen.

Chapter 26
A Story Is Not a Script

When our children were in school, sitting at the dining room table for the evening meal was a consistent ritual our family eagerly anticipated. I can vividly picture this nightly ritual. During dinner each evening our conversation usually started with a question: What was the best part of your day? Christina, in her vivid, animated way, would describe in detail the bus ride and lunch and then word-by-word everything they read in class that day. When it was Peter's turn to talk he would begin his portion of the ritual rhetoric with, "I'll say this, and then you say this . . ." and then proceed to share the script he always had in his head. I knew from the moment he could talk that he didn't think like everyone else. His mind was processing differently. Christina, on the other hand, was a pleaser of people, every teacher's dream as a student, and very much concerned about how others perceived her.

Life that is scripted might seem easier but it wouldn't be our story, my story. A scripted life would go exactly as planned; cue the lights and the entrances and exits of characters and the lines they would say and responses they would receive. Life isn't like that—it doesn't go according to my plan, and people frequently don't say or do what I might have scripted.

My story is an ordinary story, yet every time I ponder, write, or reflect on it, I learn something new about the connections I've made, who has loved me, and who I have been allowed to love. Actually, my ordinary story has played out better than any script I could have written. The parts that didn't play out according to plan have made me more compassionate, more authentic, and more human than I could have imagined.

I write my story for my own understanding, growth, and reflection and so those I love will hear the story from my voice while I still have it and while I can still remember. I write my story in the hope that it will prompt you to remember and reflect on your own story. I hope you will join me on this journey of recollection and revelry in who we are becoming as the stories unfold.

There comes a time in your life when you realize that everyone who actually remembers the day you were born is gone. These revelatory moments deserve a time of pause. Maybe you haven't given this much thought but when you do, give yourself permission to feel the emotion of the revelation. It may feel like grief or melancholy but the feeling will also be a part of the story, a snapshot of that moment in time. I still have my sister who remembers and I treasure that. I realized my children, whose story is one of adoption, don't have anyone in their lives who remembers the day they were born. I can't tell them about that day but I can tell them they are loved and prayed for and that they belong to a forever family, and that is a gift.

Sharing our stories is also a gift. The gift of a story shared is that someone who is having the same struggle can have hope. The gift is laughter in the midst of trials. The gift is grace, mercy, and forgiveness extended to yourself and others in times of failure. The gift is in the sharing of a botched but beautiful, flawed but fabulous life of lessons and love that can offer encouragement to another. Not a scripted solution but a story of heartbreak and healing. There is a gift even in the heartbreak, and when we come to the point where we can appreciate and celebrate that gift, we have embarked on a truly teachable moment.

I frequently pray for God to break my heart for what breaks His, and He is always faithful to answer that prayer. I believe His heart is broken over those who aren't extended love, grace, mercy, and forgiveness by those who claim to be His children. I believe God's heart is broken over our missed opportunities to love, forgive, and share this journey of life. That part of my story breaks my heart too. The part where I failed to forgive. The parts where I withheld grace and instead placed judgment on others. The parts where I failed to share words of love and encouragement with others.

It breaks my heart when I think that the joy I have experienced in becoming a mom was the most painful heartache of another mom's journey. It breaks my heart when I think my children never knew their grandfathers. It breaks my heart when I think of all the times I have willingly and intentionally engaged in sin that separated me from the will and the way of the sovereign Lord of the universe. This is actually what breaks God's heart the most—separation from His children. He desires a relationship with us, an honest exchange on a consistent basis. I know He still loves me even when I fail to love Him, and I marvel at the mystery of that kind of love. I know He loves you too, and I hope you will join me as we marvel in that mystery.

An unscripted life is full of mystery, things I can't understand. I can't understand the piece (peace) that seems to be missing in my children's lives. I can't make sense of the mystery of the children we've adopted becoming so fully and completely a part of us. I can't make sense of the mystery of becoming a family or of being adopted into the family of God and being an heir to the kingdom. I can't make sense of how or why He loves me, but I know I want to love others that way.

My story is not a script but a story of perseverance in the face of trials, hope in unexpected places, strength in the midst of struggles, joy in the depths of sorrow, beauty for ashes, fears conquered, and dreams realized. When I say it that way, it doesn't sound so ordinary after all. Your story is anything but ordinary as well. You are one of a kind with a story all your own, one worth pondering, picturing, and sharing.

Pictures from our past can't possibly portray the pain and pleasures we've been through together as a family, but I will continue, as long as life allows, to tell the unscripted story behind the pictures. I hope you have been prompted to do the same—ponder your own story, picture the moments, and then prepare to share.

Father, Your love is a mystery I want to continue to explore. You are holy and righteous and perfect in every way and You desire a relationship with me. That is beyond my comprehension. You have designed a way for us to have a relationship with You and with each other. Teach us to marvel in the mystery of Your love. Teach us to love one another and to treasure the gifts of each moment we share. Take each of those moments and open our eyes to see glimpses of Your glory. Show us how to share our story and how to be an encouragement to others on the same journey. Thank You most of all for Jesus. Amen.

Chapter 27
Seasonal Focus

The season of life we used to think about, talk about, and plan for is here: retirement. What did I expect? Is this it? According to Erik Erikson, the psychologist famous for his theory of psychosocial development, which identified the eight ages and eight stages of emotional/social development, I'm at the end of the generativity vs. stagnation stage, when I should be finding a way to satisfy and support the next generation (I have definitely accomplished the support half of that). My next rapidly approaching stage is integrity vs. despair, "a reflection and/or acceptance of one's life—the culmination and sense of oneself as one is and of feeling fulfilled." Yikes!

Fulfillment, culmination, reflection—okay, that last one I can handle. That's what this collection of stories is all about: reflecting and ultimately accepting that perhaps it hasn't all turned out the way I dreamed it would. Focusing on what is truly important and letting go of the rest.

I want faith to be my focus. I want to live a multifaceted but single-focused life, investing my time and energy in things that will make an eternal difference. Life is seasonal, and I feel certain that throughout my life I have been focused—just sometimes on the wrong things.

In the season of childhood I was focused on school and family with a desire to compete and win.

As a young adult I lost my focus for a season and became sidetracked by developmentally appropriate distractions of forbidden love and substance-driven 70s struggles. Thankfully, I was quick to regain my focus and set my sights on reaching the goal, or at least what I thought was the goal—graduation.

The season of marriage and parenting came along and with it came a shift in focus. The shift to a life of total focus on faith—life-changing, life-altering faith in a savior who is worthy of my total, undivided focus.

Next, a three-decade season of partnering, parenting, teaching, and investing in students' lives and focusing on making a difference for eternity.

Then came another seasonal shift: retirement, grief and loss, health concerns, and parenting adult children, and desiring to do it all with the same focus on faith in the One who has a perfect plan, the One who has placed eternity in my heart, and the One who isn't surprised by any of this.

So whether speaking and ministering to women, mentoring a child, teaching and training professional adults, listening to and advising adult children, or switching from the passenger seat to the driver's seat after my husband's stroke, I will continue to live my multifaceted, single-focused life with a focus on faith in the One who in the midst of changing seasons never changes. Abiding, not stagnating. Rejoicing, not despairing.

In my current season of life, and any season that might distract or interrupt that, I will fix my eyes on Jesus, the author and finisher of my faith, who for the joy set before Him endured the cross (Hebrews 12:2).

What have the seasons of your life looked like? Have they been satisfying or draining? As you look back, can you identify the turning points and the pivotal people in your life? Where was your focus then and where is it now or where would you like it to be? Have you grown and zeroed in on a focus that is now foundational? Take the time to draw a lifeline that represents those changes and projects forward to where you hope you are headed. What, or better yet, Who can you count on to be consistent in the midst of all of life's seasonal changes?

Father, You are the Alpha and the Omega, the beginning and the end. You alone are worthy of honor and praise. You are the One who never changes. You are the One who tells me to rest and to trust in You no matter what the surrounding circumstances may look like. Help me to grow closer to You and help me to change to be more like You. Help me to give grace and mercy because I have received Your grace and mercy. Thank you most of all for Jesus. Amen.

Chapter 28
A Porch Perspective

I love my porch and the new perspective it brings every time I sit and look out on the lake. Still water and a gentle breeze bring clarity, calm, and peace where there has been confusion and chaos. This backyard has hosted celebrations beginning with our wedding decades ago on a very warm July afternoon following a cleansing morning rain. Since then there have been annual Easter egg hunts and Fourth of July BBQs, Thanksgiving and Christmas gatherings, and neighborhood block parties. We have gathered to remember after funerals and hosted graduation and milestone anniversary celebrations, but the best times are the dailies. The daily breakfast and devotions together, the daily afternoon coffee and nap, and the daily sunset dinners and debriefing of the day in the best waterfront venue in town.

We've lived here in excess of four decades and we didn't always have a porch. I often wonder why we waited so long to add the porch, and the year we finally did was the year of the hurricanes. No sooner had we finished the addition then we heard the news of impending storms and figured it would wipe out our new addition, but we were spared. It has become my favorite room in the house, and even in the heat of the summer, you will find me there, under the fan, enjoying the backyard birds and bunnies. The view has changed over the years. The children's play equipment, minus the swings and slide, has become the garden arbor, and a potted plant deck has improved the side view. Gnomes of many faces and yard art collected from vintage treasure hunts make me smile. The signage on the fence of our street name from a construction site, the piece of an old florist sign that now just says "Flor," and a custom-made sign that was a retirement gift from the city are also reminders of times gone by.

I am not a gardener and I go more for the natural look than the carefully manicured pristine approach. Anything green is good, and the ferns and little yellow daisies at the lake's edge are among my favorites. We have never had a dock or a boat except the small paddleboat that has served us well over the years. I enjoy looking out on the water at all times of the day as the reflection of the tall trees is another visible marker of time that has passed, and I spend time reflecting. I love these trees, all fifty-two of them, and the shade and shadows they provide. I know there are fifty-two because I trimmed around them all once (and once was enough) on my knees. I love the flower-producing weeds that grow at the lake's edge. I love the natural gnomes produced by the cypress knees along the shore. I love the memories of children's laughter in the lake on rafts and the impromptu picnics in the yard. I love the family photos taken each year in front of the same tree to measure the growth.

The writing somehow becomes richer in the afternoon hours with a gentle breeze blowing on the porch. There has been much soul searching and prayer journaling, letter writing and reading, and even some solving of national problems, though no one has ever come to me in search of those solutions. I am not sure what will come next but I am sure the porch will be a part of the process. It s a place where relationships have been nurtured, but mostly it is a place of renewal, offering the opportunity to recharge and restore order while observing God's perfect order in creation. He sends the rain to refresh and replenish a parched land. He sends visible reminders of His faithfulness in each sunrise and sunset to replenish and refresh a parched soul.

Is there something you are waiting to do like we waited to add our porch? Don't wait. Do it now, enjoy it now. You don't need a porch for this process but you do need a place. Where is your place? Be intentional about creating a place to recharge and reflect. It could be a closet repurposed or a quiet corner of a room. Do you have some visible reminders of time gone by that prompt memories of both the pain and the pleasure? God wants to comfort you and also to remind you that He has provided all creation for you to enjoy. His invisible qualities are made visible in creation, so take some time today to take it all in and enjoy the work of His Hand.

Father, You are the master craftsman, the creator of it all. You put a new song in our hearts. You created us to glorify and enjoy You. Open our eyes today to see all that You have for us. Cause us to remember Your faithfulness in every season of our lives and Your mercies that are new every morning. You rejoice over us with singing, and the birds of the air remind us of Your song. You have a purpose in the pain and the pleasure. Give us perfect rest and restore and replenish our souls. Guide our steps and direct us in the way we should go. Thank you most of all for Jesus. Amen.

Chapter 29
If I Had My Life to Live Over

I believe self-assessment is a key ingredient in a life well lived, so I welcomed an assignment in a writing class that involved a response to the question: If I had my life to live over, what would I do differently?

As part of the assignment, I interviewed some of the people who matter the most to me. Their responses were spontaneous and exactly what I expected. Here are the things they said I should do differently if I had my life to live over:

- My husband said, "Stop trying to please everyone and take time to rest"— of course I know he's right.
- My son said, "Ride more roller coasters"—chances of this are slim to none, but I did say I'd try to be more adventurous.
- My daughter said, "Relax and not be so uptight"—this is also a goal worth pursuing.

And I say, in response to their advice and my own inner desires, if I had my life to live over again, I would:

- write more letters and send more cards
- get up earlier and stay up later (suck the marrow out of every day)
- make exercise a part of my daily routine
- worry less and trust God more
- share my faith with everyone who would listen
- take more road trips
- eat more fish
- take a 2:00 latte break everyday
- watch more sunsets
- sit on the porch longer
- plant a garden and enjoy it
- read more great books and watch less TV
- spend more time with children and senior citizens
- delve deeper and listen longer to family members and friends
- give more attention to detail
- be a more faithful friend
- ask for and accept help from others
- take time for a weekly treasure hunt
- compliment more than I complain
- simplify when it comes to stuff
- journal the journey
- use the good dishes every day and entertain more often

If I had my life to live over I would:
> spend more time listening and learning from the people who enrich my life
> start writing my stories sooner

What would your list look like? Whose advice would you solicit? Whose advice would you heed? How are you currently stewarding your time? Consider the concept of spending, wasting, or investing time and how they are different. Will you choose to see each day as an opportunity to begin again?

Father, You are the giver of life. Every day is a gift, an opportunity to do things over and to make the most of the time You have given. Teach us to number our days and to choose to steward our time and invest it in activities that will make a difference for eternity. Give us eyes to see and ears to hear the messages You have for us. Thank you most of all for Jesus. Amen.

Conclusion

As I come to the final chapter, I want to return to the words I have emphasized throughout this collection of life stories: *relationship, rescue,* and *renewal.*

We have talked about relationships with family, friends, spouse, siblings, colleagues, and confidants, and while all those relationships are important, only one relationship is essential for us to experience that rescue and renewal we all so desperately desire. Only one relationship gives us our identity and only one relationship will never disappoint.

We were created by God and for God. He desires a relationship with each one of us. Our relationship with God was broken by sin, and when a relationship is broken, reconciliation is necessary. God provided that reconciliation in the form of His Son, Jesus. He sent His one and only Son into the world to provide a way for us to have that relationship restored. He sent Jesus to rescue us from sin and shame and to renew a right relationship with Him.

Jesus was born of a virgin, grew to be a man, and willingly went to the cross to pay the penalty for my sin. The Bible says, "For God so loved the world that he gave his one and only Son, that whoever believes in him shall not perish but have eternal life" (John 3:16). Jesus was crucified, died, and was buried, and on the third day He rose again and now sits at the right hand of the Father interceding for—speaking up for, standing up for—me, as an advocate to the Father.

God desires a relationship with me. He has adopted me into His family. He gave me the right to become a child of God. He rescued me from the penalty of my sin and has made me a brand-new creation. That is a story worth sharing. That is a story I know to be true because I have that relationship. I have experienced that rescue. I am that brand-new, renewed creation.

He wants the same for you. God wants a relationship with you. He made a way for you to be in relationship with Him through His Son, Jesus. When you acknowledge and admit your sin and believe that Jesus paid the penalty for your sin on the cross, and when you believe that He died and was buried and on the third day He rose again, and when you confess with your mouth—tell others about how He rescued you and how you have become a new creation—you are renewed and your purpose becomes clear and your desires line up with His desires for you.

So, as I close, I ask you, would you like to have a relationship with Jesus? Would you like to accept the rescue He has already paid for? Would you like to have a relationship with the One who will never disappoint, the One who will never leave you or forsake you? Would you like to be celebrating the journey with the assurance of an eternal destination? All you need to do is tell Him the desire of your heart and He will rescue you and give you that renewal you've been searching for, that brand-new start.

You can pray a simple prayer like this:

Dear Jesus, I do believe You are the Son of God and that You came to pay the penalty for my sin on the cross. I believe You died and that You were buried and on the third day You rose again. I now turn from my sin and turn to You. Fill me with Your Holy Spirit to begin a brand-new life. Amen.

If you made this decision, please share your story. Thank you for allowing me to share mine. I'd love to hear from you and celebrate the journey of this renewed life with you.

NOTES

1. Dr Seuss (Theodor Seuss Geisel), *Oh, the Places You'll Go* (New York: Random House, 1990), 44.
2. Malcolm Jones, "The History and Lost Art of Letter Writing," *Newsweek*, January 17, 2009, www.newsweek.com.

ABOUT THE AUTHOR

Becky is a repurposed teacher with a lifetime of experience relating to people of every age and stage. Her enthusiasm is contagious as she shares a message of hope and life. Her motto is, "Celebrate the journey; don't wait for the destination" and her pictures from the past have become possibilities for the future.

Wife to Pete and mother to Christina and Peter, treasure hunter and upcycler, lover of the afternoon latte and a great read, she can be found most days on her back porch.

Becky is available to speak for retreats, luncheons, and other events, and to lead workshops and times of prayer.

Please contact her at:
Email: beckyburgue@yahoo.com
Phone: 813-961-2810
Website: www.beckyburgue.com
Facebook: http://www.Facebook.com/Celebrate-the-Journey-Don't-Wait-for-the-Destination